THE
BREAD MACHINE
BOOK

THE
BREAD MACHINE
BOOK

OVER 100 RECIPES FOR EASY-TO-MAKE,

SPECTACULAR BREADS

MARJIE LAMBERT

APPLE

Dedicated to Sarah, Diane and Beverly

A QUINTET BOOK

Published by The Apple Press
6 Blundell Street
London N7 9BH

ISBN 1-85076-657-6

This book was designed and produced by
Quintet Publishing Limited
6 Blundell Street
London N7 9BH

Creative Director: Richard Dewing
Designers: Ian Hunt, Linda Henley
Project Editor: Alison Bravington
Editor: Janet Swarbrick
Home Economist: Janet Brinkworth
Photographer: David Armstrong

Typeset in Great Britain by
Central Southern Typesetters, Eastbourne
Manufactured in Malaysia by
C. H. Colour Scan Sdn. Bhd.
Printed in Singapore by
Star Standard Industries (Pte) Ltd

The publishers would like to thank
Panasonic for their help and for the loan
of a bread machine to create the
breads photographed.

CONTENTS

INTRODUCTION

This is a secret that for years I've tried to share with friends who cook, but it was a secret no one believed: baking bread is fun and easy. Time-consuming, yes. Messy, definitely. Kneading, while mentally relaxing, will tire your muscles. But difficult? No.

Bread dough is patient, flexible, and tolerant of mistakes. The rewards are wonderful – the fragrance, the texture, the taste of fresh-baked bread are unbeatable. But because people are often intimidated by the mysteries of yeast, bread-making at home has been in danger of becoming a lost art.

Using a bread machine, baking bread becomes one of the easiest tasks in the kitchen, yet it produces spectacular results. You don't have to worry that water will be too cold to activate yeast, or so hot that it kills it: the bread machine regulates the temperature. You won't be kneading dough until your muscles ache: the bread machine will do all the kneading for you. There's no need to worry that draughts from the air-conditioning unit will interfere with rising dough: the dough is protected while it's inside the machine. From a dark, dense pumpernickel to feather-light white bread to a sweet panettone, making a delicious array of breads is no more work than simply measuring out the ingredients. And since most machines have timers, the ingredients can be measured into the bread tin just before you go to bed and the freshly cooked bread will be hot when you wake up.

With a bread machine, you can create an infinite variety of loaves to suit your tastes, your store cupboard and the season. Substitute dried cranberries for raisins in a Christmas bread, add cracked wheat to a favourite bread to give it more fibre, or decorate a plaited loaf with the slivered almonds left over from another baking project. You no longer have to settle for ordinary bread.

Bread machines do have their flaws. Most are inflexible in their kneading, rising and baking cycles; they purée fruits and nuts that are added at the beginning of the kneading cycle; and they have little tolerance for dough that is particularly stiff or soft. But the newer models have different settings for different varieties of bread – whole-wheat bread needs more time to rise than white bread; sweet breads need less baking time.

And if your bread machine still doesn't give you enough flexibility, you can just let the machine do the kneading, then remove it from the machine and let it rise and bake according to your timetable.

GETTING TO KNOW YOUR MACHINE

Mastering bread-machine baking is like getting to know the quirks and idiosyncrasies of any new piece of equipment. Some machines knead longer than others or allow longer rising time. Some bread tins have different capacities than others, although they are labelled as the same size. Some models require a little more liquid or yeast than others. Flour absorbs varying amounts of liquid depending on the weather. The dough reacts differently to water that is highly acidic or alkaline.

To get accustomed to a new machine or this book, start with a simple recipe, such as basic white bread, and see how it comes out. If you have any problems refer to the Troubleshooting Guide on pages 14–15.

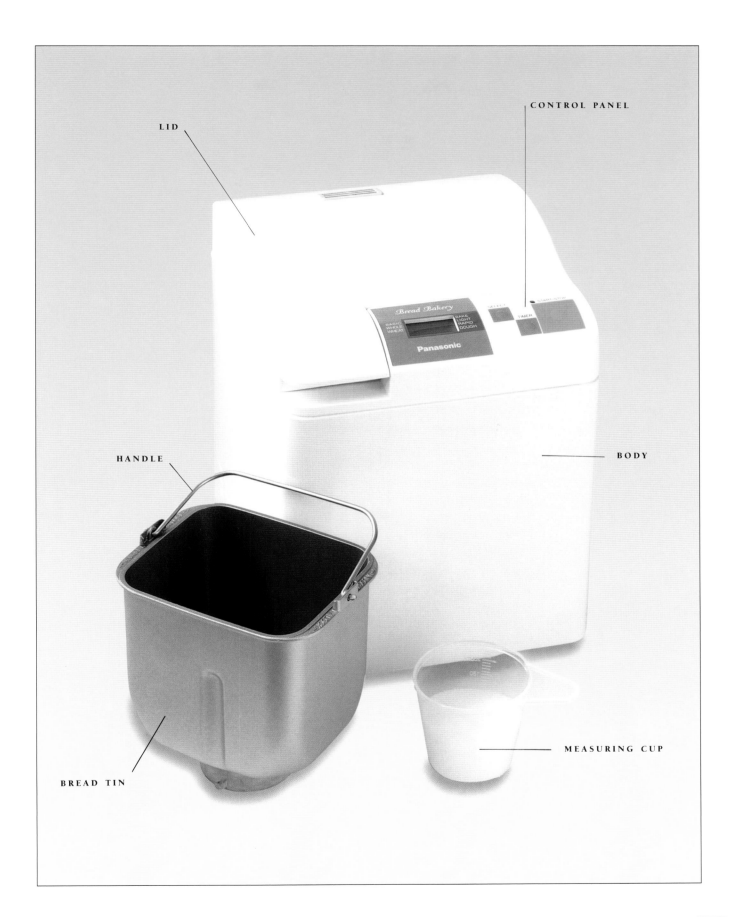

LID

CONTROL PANEL

HANDLE

BODY

BREAD TIN

MEASURING CUP

BAKING BREAD

Before you start, assemble all the ingredients. Be sure that the yeast is fresh. All ingredients should be at room temperature. Cold liquids and butter can be heated in the microwave (I usually add the butter to the liquid and heat them together). Hold a cold egg in your hand for five minutes or so while you review the recipe, or put it in a bowl of water no hotter than 27°C/80°F. Although frozen yeast should be given time to come to room temperature, yeast that has been stored in the refrigerator will come to room temperature quickly enough without special treatment. Never put yeast in the microwave.

Be sure the kneading paddle is well seated in the bottom of the tin. Add the ingredients in the order suggested by the manufacturer's instructions. This may vary from one machine to the next. If you are using a timer, the order may change, see "Using the Timer," below. Fix the bread tin securely into the bread machine. Select settings on the control panel according to the manufacturer's instructions and press Start.

To check the dough while the bread is kneading, look for it to form a fairly smooth ball that is a bit tacky to the touch and settles only slightly when the paddle stops kneading. If, after the ingredients are mixed, the imprint of the paddle remains in the dough and the edges look a little jagged, add more liquid. Start with one tablespoon, then add additional liquid one teaspoon at a time, giving the dough time to absorb the liquid before adding more. If the dough is so soft that it loses its shape as soon as the paddle pauses, add more flour, one tablespoon at a time. Although these instructions fit most breads, some breads are designed to have dough that is a little stiffer or softer. Don't be shy about keeping the lid up and watching at this stage. It is only when the bread is in the rising and baking stages that an open lid will interfere with temperature controls.

When the bread is done, remove it from the machine and the baking tin immediately. Otherwise, the steam released by the bread will condense in the tin, making the bread soggy on the outside. The bread should be allowed to cool for 20 to 30 minutes before you slice into it.

The kneading paddle should be well seated in the bottom of the bread tin

Add ingredients in the order suggested by the manufacturer

The bread tin should be securely seated inside the machine

ADDITIONS

Fruit and vegetables added at the beginning of the knead cycle will be puréed or shredded into tiny bits. If you want the raisins to remain whole or other fruit to remain in chunks, add it 10 to 15 minutes into the kneading cycle. Most machines now have a beeper that signals when it's time to add the additions.

If you are using the timer to make the bread and have no choice but to add all ingredients at the beginning, consider the moisture content of the additions. Juicy dried apricots or roasted red peppers may add as much as one or two tablespoons of juice if they go through the entire kneading process. Also, because too much sugar can interfere with the yeast, high-sugar additions like candied fruit should be added late in the kneading cycle.

USING THE TIMER

If you are using the bread machine timer so that the mixing will be delayed, the ingredients should be layered so the yeast does not come into contact with liquids prematurely. Generally, you should put the liquids in first, followed by the dry ingredients and the yeast last. Salt and wheat germ may also interfere with the yeast if any significant quantities are in prolonged contact with the yeast.

Recipes containing perishable ingredients such as eggs or cottage cheese should not be made using the timer, unless the delay is only an hour or so. You can substitute water and powdered milk for whole milk (use three tablespoons of dry milk per 250 ml/8 fl oz), but the dry milk should be layered with the other dry ingredients so that it does not come in contact with the water prematurely. I have not had any trouble using small quantities of butter in bread made overnight. However, if you wish you can substitute vegetable oil for butter.

OVEN-BAKED BREAD

Any of the breads in this cookbook can be baked in a conventional oven. I use a 24 cm (9½ in) loaf tin for most breads. The 675 g (1½ lb) breads made with bread flour may require a larger tin. The 450 g (1 lb) breads that include rye or low-gluten flours can be cooked in the 24 cm (9½ in) tin, but will rise higher and look more attractive in a 21.5 cm (8½ in) tin. Unless otherwise indicated, most breads should be baked at 180°C/350°F/Gas 4 for 30 to 35 minutes.

A cautionary note about baking sheets and bread tins: many of the tins available today are of a construction or material that changes the cooking conditions. Double-layered tins with an insulating air cushion protect against scorching, but bread cooked in these tins will take longer to bake. Some of the heavy, expensive tins with black surfaces will brown the bread faster and require lower baking temperatures and/or shorter baking times. If you use a glass loaf tin, reduce the oven temperature by 4°C/25°F/Gas ½.

ABOVE Bagels (page 85)

BREAD BAKING INGREDIENTS

People have been baking bread since prehistoric times, beginning with an unleavened bread made of meal ground from corns or beechnuts and mixed with water. The first leavened bread is believed to have been baked by the Egyptians about 4,000 BC. Some dough left out for hours captured wild yeast from the air. When the dough was put on the hearth to bake, it puffed up. That was the first sourdough, although bakers went to great lengths to minimize the sour taste while taking advantage of its leavening qualities. Later, bakers discovered a yeasty byproduct of beer brewing that did not create such a sour taste. It was not until the 19th century that compressed yeast was perfected.

In basic bread the yeast, activated by warm water and fed by sugar, ferments. It creates tiny bubbles of carbon dioxide gas that makes the dough rise. Gluten, an elastic protein in the dough, stretches and holds in the gas bubbles. The more gluten in the flour, the better the bread will rise.

FLOUR

Barley, millet, oats, rye and wheat have been milled for thousands of years in Europe and Asia. Corn was a grain of the Americas. Only wheat and, to a lesser extent, rye, have the gluten necessary to make leavened bread. The other grains should be used in combination with wheat flour to make bread.

WHEAT FLOURS

Wheat flours, the most commonly used flours, are milled from the wheat berry. The berry consists of three parts: the outer hull, or bran; the small germ or embryo inside; and the endosperm, a starchy material that feeds the embryo.

White flour – including bread flour and all-purpose flour – consists of the milled endosperm, with the bran and germ removed. All-purpose flour is milled to be used in a variety of ways and is made with a combination of hard and soft wheats. Bread flour, milled specifically for bread, is made only from hard wheat. Bread flour has a higher gluten content and will absorb more liquid. Bread made with bread flour will rise significantly higher than bread made with all-purpose flour.

Whole-wheat flour contains the bran, germ and endosperm of the wheat berry. It has proportionately less gluten than bread flour or all-purpose flour. It rises more slowly and not as high. It may also have a slightly bitter flavour. For those reasons, many whole-wheat breads are made with a combination of whole-wheat and white flours. Some bakers add wheat gluten for a higher loaf.

Graham flour, named after Dr Sylvester Graham, a 19th century health food devotee, is a coarsely ground whole-wheat flour milled from soft winter wheat. It has less gluten than whole-wheat flour and will not rise as high. The quality of graham flour varies widely. Some manufacturers package inferior flour with wheat bran and label it graham flour.

Semolina flour is a high-gluten white flour milled from durum or hard winter wheat. It is most often used in pasta (and may be labelled pasta flour). It makes a delicious bread when used with other flour. By itself, it makes a heavy loaf.

Triticale is a man-made grain, a hybrid of rye and wheat. It is a high-protein grain with the hardiness of rye and the gluten of wheat, although it is best combined with wheat flour. The grain was created with the intent of cultivating it in difficult growing conditions in poorer parts of the world.

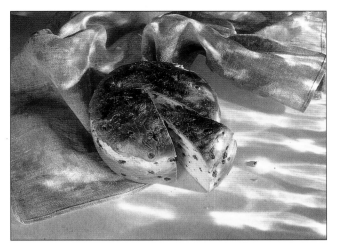

ABOVE Panettone (page 123)

NON-WHEAT FLOURS

Non-wheat flours are low in gluten or gluten-free and should be used in combination with wheat flours unless you require gluten-free bread for health reasons.

Rye is a hardy grain that grows well in cold, wet climates where wheat does not. That's why so many Scandinavian and Russian breads are rye breads. Rye flour contains some gluten, but must be mixed with wheat flour. Medium or light rye flour consists only of the endosperm. Dark rye and pumpernickel are milled from the bran, germ and endosperm of the rye berry and are coarser, darker flours. Its grind and content may vary; some manufacturers market a blend of whole wheat and dark rye as pumpernickel.

Amaranth flour was a staple of the Aztecs. It has a nutty, slightly spicy flavour. It is higher in protein than most flours, but is low in gluten.

Barley flour, milled from a grain that dates back to the Stone Age, has a slightly sweet taste, a soft texture and a low gluten content.

Buckwheat flour is made from the triangular seeds of a cereal grass. It adds a pungent, earthy flavour to bread. It is a high-fat flour, low in gluten.

Corn flour, milled from the whole kernel of corn, adds a sweet flavour to bread. It is gluten-free. Corn starch and the British cornflour are milled only from the endosperm.

Millet flour, milled since Neolithic times and a staple food in parts of Africa and Asia, adds a yellowish colour and a pleasantly gritty texture to bread. It is low in gluten.

Oat flour, made from oats that have been ground into powder, is very low in gluten and must be mixed with wheat flour, but is high in protein.

Quinoa flour, an ancient pearly grain from Peru, gives bread a nutty flavour. It is very high in protein but is gluten-free.

Rice flour, the flour most commonly used in gluten-free breads, is milled from either white or brown rice. It makes bread with a sweet flavour and chewy texture. Brown rice flour includes the bran.

Soya flour gives bread a moist texture and is very high in protein, but should be used sparingly because it adds a slight bitter flavour. It is gluten-free.

GRAINS

A few of these grains are easily found in grocery stores, but most will be found only in health food stores. They will add taste and texture to bread, but will not contribute to its rising. They should be added in small quantities, typically 2 to 4 tablespoons for a 450 g (1 lb) loaf.

WHEAT

Many forms of wheat are available as grains. The wheat berry is the whole grain and it is much too hard to eat as it is. It can be softened by sprouting (the berry is soaked in water that is changed at least twice a day for several days) or by cooking (the berry is boiled with lots of water for an hour).

Cracked wheat is the wheat berry that has been broken into pieces, but is still too hard to eat without cooking. It can be softened by boiling for 30 to 40 minutes.

Bulgur is a wheat berry that has been steamed and cracked. It adds crunch to bread. To cook bulgur, boil in water for six minutes and drain thoroughly.

Wheat bran, the outer hull of the grain, is also known as miller's bran or unprocessed bran flakes. It interferes with the elasticity of gluten and should be used in small quantities.

Wheat germ is the embryo of the wheat berry. It is high in nutrients, has a nutty flavour, and is high in oils which can cause it to turn rancid if it is not kept refrigerated.

Bran cereal, such as bran flakes or All-Bran, are made with wheat bran and other ingredients, including sugar and salt, and may be toasted. They add good flavour and texture to bread.

OTHER GRAINS

Cornmeal, milled from corn, adds a sweet flavour and, if uncooked, a crumbly texture. It can interfere with the gluten, so should be used in small quantities unless it is cooked or softened in boiling water first.

Millet, widely known as birdseed, can be added to bread in small amounts in its whole, unhulled state.

Oatmeal, the most nutritious of the cereal grasses, means old-fashioned rolled oats in this cookbook. The husk is removed and the grain is sliced, steamed and rolled. The dried oats may have trouble absorbing thicker liquids such as apple sauce or buttermilk. In this cookbook, most recipes using those liquids call for a little boiling water to be poured over the oatmeal before other ingredients are added.

Oat bran is the hull of the oat and is high in soluble fibre. Oat bran can interfere with the gluten in bread dough and should be used in small quantities, between 60 ml (2 fl oz) and 125 ml (4 fl oz) for a 450 g (1 lb) loaf.

YEAST

Yeast is a living organism that is activated when it comes in contact with warm liquids. It ferments most readily when it has sugar to feed on, which is why most bread recipes contain at least a teaspoon of sugar. However, it will also feed on flour.

In this book, yeast means active dry yeast. I had the best results with a yeast made specifically for bread machines and sold in 100 g (4 oz) jars. Yeast in pre-measured envelopes also worked, although the bread did not rise as high. I also tested a rapid-rise yeast and it worked nicely on the bread machine's rapid-bake cycle, but it rose the least of all four yeasts I tested. Because the whole-wheat flour needs a longer rising period, I wouldn't recommend using a quick-rise yeast when you make whole-wheat bread.

SALT

Salt is critical in bread. It strengthens the gluten. Salt-free bread may rise nicely, but will then collapse. However, salt in high concentrations also inhibits the yeast's rising action. Salt and yeast should never be added so that they come in contact with each other prior to mixing. Because some sodium is necessary for bread, most salt substitutes cannot be used.

SWEETENERS

Yeast ferments best when it feeds on sugar. Sugar also acts as a preservative and contributes to the golden colour of the crust. But too much sugar will interfere with the yeast's rising action and cause the bread to collapse. Most yeast breads and rolls are not very sweet, even if they are dessert breads. Dessert breads usually get their sweetness from a glaze, dry sugar topping, or another addition which is made after baking.

The addition of candied fruit is a particular problem with bread machines. When candied fruit is used, it is usually in breads that already have several tablespoons of sweetener. The kneading will shred the candied fruit and release more sugar into the dough. Candied fruit should be added late in the kneading cycle, or kneaded in by hand if the bread is to be baked in the oven.

Sugar also scorches easily. A growing number of machines have a special setting with shorter cooking times for sweet breads. If your machine does not have a sweet-bread setting, choose the light-crust option.

In small quantities – 1 or 2 tablespoons – sugar, brown sugar, honey and molasses can be substituted for each other in equal amounts. Sugar and brown sugar can always be substituted for each other. Tablespoon for tablespoon, most honeys are slightly sweeter than sugar. If the recipe calls for more than two tablespoons of sweetener, substitute two parts honey for three parts sugar (e.g., 2 tablespoons of honey for 3 tablespoons of sugar). Molasses is not as sweet as sugar. When substituting more than two tablespoons, use four parts molasses for three parts sugar. Confectioner's sugar contains cornstarch and should not be used as a substitute.

Less commonly used sweeteners in bread are maple syrup and corn syrup. Maple syrup can be substituted in equal quantities. Corn syrup is not as sweet as sugar and should be substituted with two parts corn syrup for one part sugar.

Liquid forms of sugar, including honey, molasses, corn syrup and maple syrup, should be counted toward the total liquid content of the ingredients. If the substitution involves substituting a dry form for a liquid form, or vice versa, you will need to adjust the liquid ingredients accordingly.

LIQUIDS

The variety of liquids used in bread-baking is nearly infinite. Most common are water, milk, buttermilk, eggs, beer, and potato water, but don't be surprised to come across recipes that list wine, orange juice, or other liquids. Sour cream, yogurt and cottage cheese should be counted as liquids, although their consistencies differ and the amount of other liquid needed may vary. Puréed fruit and vegetables such as apple sauce and mashed potatoes also contain some liquid. Water that potatoes have been cooked in adds flavour, nutrients and a softer texture to bread.

Water will give the bread a crisper crust. Most tap water is fine, but soft (acidic) water may produce soft, sticky dough and hard (alkaline) water will interfere with the fermentation of the yeast.

Milk will give the bread a softer crust and more golden colour. You can substitute equal amounts of whole, skimmed and non-fat milk for each other. Powdered non-fat milk is very helpful in bread-baking, particularly when the bread is being baked on a timer and the ingredients will be sitting at room temperature overnight. Powdered milk is also used when the recipe calls for another liquid – such as beer or apple sauce – but you still want a golden colour and softer crust. Use 3 tablespoons of powdered milk per 250 ml (9 fl oz) of liquid.

Buttermilk will give the bread a tender crumb and a hint of tangy flavour. It also adds to the acidity of the dough and may need to be neutralized with a pinch of baking soda.

EGGS

Eggs give bread a softer crust and richer flavour and contribute to the leavening. In this cookbook, breads were tested using large eggs, which are equal to about 60 ml (2 fl oz) of liquid. I generally avoided recipes that call for only part of an egg, and increased other liquids by 2 tablespoons instead. When the bread's eggy character is important, though, recipes will call for an extra yolk. Breads containing eggs should not be made on a timer unless the delay is no more than one hour.

FATS

Fats are used sparingly in most breads, but are important. They act as preservatives and give a tender texture. French bread goes stale quickly because it uses no fat. Butter, margarine, vegetable oil, shortening and lard can be used interchangeably. In small quantities there will be no noticeable difference. If you are substituting more than one tablespoon of a solid fat for a liquid fat or vice versa, the amount of other liquid in the dough will have to be adjusted.

Lard gives bread a slightly flakier texture and crustier finish. I don't like to use margarine because it can contain water. If you're watching cholesterol and want a substitute for butter, use vegetable oil. You can substitute olive oil, but in quantities less than three tablespoons, you are not likely to notice a difference in taste, especially if you're not using extra-virgin olive oil. Speciality oils, such as sesame and walnut oil, are strongly flavoured and should be used sparingly.

If you want to cut every bit of fat out of your bread, you can substitute apple sauce or puréed prunes. Puréed fruit contains some liquid, so the amount of other liquid in the recipe may have to be reduced.

Butter should always be brought to room temperature before the dough is kneaded. Soft butter mixes more evenly. This is especially critical in high-fat breads like brioche.

A note about greasing baking sheets or tins: use butter or solid vegetable shortening. Oil will soak into the dough. Some margarines may scorch.

TROUBLESHOOTING GUIDE

TOO MUCH OR TOO LITTLE LIQUID

The most frequent cause of trouble with bread made in a bread machine is too much or too little liquid. Keep in mind that flour absorbs moisture from the air. That's why a loaf of bread may turn out perfect one time and awful the next. In humid weather, the flour may have already absorbed an extra 1 or 2 tablespoons of moisture. If you add the usual amount of liquid, it may mushroom and collapse, or develop a coarse, holey texture. Likewise, if the climate is very dry, the four may need a little extra moisture, or it will have a dense, heavy texture or a gnarled top.

Check the dough about 10 minutes into the kneading cycle. The dough should be smooth, soft and slightly tacky. It should settle just the slightest bit but hold its shape when the kneading paddle stops. If the dough is very soft, settles quickly when the kneading paddle stops and can't hold its shape, add 1 tablespoon of flour. If the dough is stiff with ragged edges and imprints of the paddle remain in the dough for more than a couple of seconds, add 1 tablespoon of liquid.

TEMPERATURE

Ingredients should be at room temperature. But "room temperature" may be too hot or too cold in particularly hot or cold weather. If the ingredients are too cold, they may not activate the yeast soon enough. If they are too warm – such as on a hot day in a kitchen that is not air-conditioned – the yeast may cause the dough to rise too much and overflow the machine.

ADDING FRUIT AND VEGETABLES

Another variable that can put too much liquid into the dough is fruit or vegetables. If fruit or vegetables are added at the beginning of the kneading cycle, they will be ground up and release more liquid than if they were added at the beeper or after the first kneading. If you're using the timer to knead the bread, have to add fruit or vegetables at the beginning and can't check the dough during the kneading, reduce liquids by 1 to 2 teaspoons for drier additions like raisins or sun-dried tomatoes, and by 1 to 2 tablespoons for wetter additions, like shredded apple or roasted red peppers.

PROBLEMS AND ANSWERS

BREAD COLLAPSED

- Too much liquid. Next time reduce liquid by 2 tablespoons, then monitor the dough as it kneads and adjust liquid or flour for a firm but sticky dough.
- You omitted the salt or used a salt substitute. The gluten needs some salt to support it as it rises. Minimum amount is ½ teaspoon for a 450 g (1 lb) loaf, ¾ teaspoon for a 675 g (1½ lb) loaf. Most salt substitutes will not work.
- Too much sugar. Decrease by 1 tablespoon next time. You're getting into dangerous territory with more than 40 g (1½ oz) sugar for a 450 g (1 lb) loaf, 6 tablespoons for a 675 g (1½ lb) loaf, although some recipes will work with more. Don't forget that sugary additions like candied fruit increase the quantity of sugar.

BREAD HAS BURNED CRUST, BUT CENTRE IS FINE

- Too much sugar can cause the crust to burn. Set controls for sweet bread and/or light crust. If it still burns – or your machine does not have those settings – reduce sugar (or other sweetener) or by 1 tablespoon. Or remove the bread 5 minutes before the machine is done. Or bake the bread in a loaf tin in a conventional oven.

BREAD NOT BAKED IN CENTRE

- Too much liquid or not enough flour. Next time, reduce liquid by 1 to 2 tablespoons or increase flour by 2 to 4 tablespoons (if the bread tin has room for a larger loaf); then monitor dough as it kneads, and adjust flour or liquid for a firm but sticky dough. The bread machine has little tolerance for dough that varies much from a set ratio of liquid to flour. Often, those same breads – especially sweet breads like kugelhopf or panettone – will turn out fine when baked in a conventional oven. Set the bread machine to make dough, then remove it, punch it down, and put it in a buttered loaf tin. Let it rise in a warm place for 45 minutes to 1 hour, then bake at 190°C (375°F) for about 30 minutes.
- If it is a sweet bread and has sticky pockets, reduce the sugar or sweetener by 1 tablespoon.

TROUBLESHOOTING GUIDE

BREAD HAS GNARLED TOP AND/OR HEAVY, DENSE TEXTURE

- Not enough liquid or too much flour. If the bread tin has room for a larger loaf, add 1 to 2 tablespoons of liquid next time, otherwise reduce flour by 2 to 4 tablespoons. Monitor dough as it kneads and adjust liquid or flour for a firm but sticky texture. (Note: If you tap the measuring cup several times to get flour to settle, you may be cramming too much flour into the measuring cup.)

- Too much low-gluten flour. Breads that consist entirely of rye or, to a lesser extent, whole-wheat flour will be dense and heavy. Sometimes, this is desirable. If it is not, substitute bread flour for part of the rye or whole-wheat flour. Or add wheat gluten, an additive available at health food stores.

- Too many extras, such as oatmeal, wheat germ, fruit or nuts substituted for flour. If there is room in your bread tin, add 2 oz (50 g) bread flour and about 2 tablespoons of liquid. Otherwise, reduce the extras.

- Dry grains soaked up too much liquid. Oatmeal is a particular offender. Add 1 to 2 tablespoons of liquid.

BREAD HAS MUSHROOM TOP WITH AIR UNDERNEATH, OR HAS TUNNELS OR COARSE HOLEY TEXTURE

- Too much liquid. Next time reduce the amount of liquid by 1 to 2 tablespoons, then monitor the dough as it kneads and adjust the amount of liquid or flour for a firm but sticky dough.

- Too much yeast. Reduce yeast by ¼ teaspoon for a smaller loaf, ½ teaspoon for a larger loaf.

BREAD RISES TOO MUCH

- Too much yeast. Reduce the amount of yeast by ½ teaspoon next time.

- Too much liquid, especially if there are large air pockets in bread. Reduce liquid by 1 to 2 tablespoons next time, check kneading and adjust flour for firm, sticky texture.

- You omitted the salt. Salt supports the gluten and stops it collapsing, but it also stops the yeast rising too high.

BREAD DOESN'T RISE ENOUGH

- Not enough yeast. Increase yeast by ½ teaspoon next time.

- Yeast is not fresh. Proof by putting 2 teaspoons of yeast in 125 ml (4 fl oz) warm water 40.5 to 46°C (105 to 115°F). If it does not develop a thick head of foam in 5 to 10 minutes, discard the yeast.

- You're using rapid-rise yeast or the rapid-rise cycle. The price for this shortcut is a loaf that doesn't rise as high.

- You're using yeast that does not do well in bread machines. Switch to yeast produced specifically for bread machines.

- You used hot liquid – over 46°C (115°F) – and it killed the yeast.

- Not enough liquid. Increase liquid by 1 tablespoon next time.

- Too much sugar (honey, molasses, etc) may be interfering with yeast. If it is a high-sugar bread (or if it has sugary additions like candied fruit), reduce sugar by 1 tablespoon, or increase yeast by ¼ teaspoon. Conversely, yeast works better when there is at least 1 teaspoon of sugar to feed it. Although some recipes, such as French Bread, get along without it, the yeast rises better with a small amount of sweetener.

- You're using too much low-gluten flour. Increase the proportion of white flour. Or substitute bread flour for all-purpose flour.

- Your tap water is too hard (alkaline). Add 1 teaspoon of lemon juice or vinegar.

- Too much salt. This may be because you added salty extras, like salted nuts, without reducing the amount of salt.

- You allowed the salt and yeast to come in contact with each other prior to mixing. A high concentration of salt in direct contact with yeast can kill the yeast.

- You opened the lid during the rising stage and allowed warm air to escape.

BREAD DOESN'T RISE AT ALL AND IS A STICKY OR BURNT LAYERED MESS

- You forgot to set the paddle in the pan, or it was not firmly seated and came loose.

Basic Breads

Basic White Bread	Potato Bread
17	25
Honey Wheat Bread	Graham Bread
17	26
Egg Bread	Rye Bread
18	27
Sour Cream Cornmeal Bread	Cornmeal Yeast Bread
18	28
Onion Dill Rye Bread	Buttermilk Oatmeal Bread
20	28
Light Rye Bread	Italian Herb Bread
20	30
Pumpernickel Bread	Orange Cumin Bread
22	31
Buttermilk Pumpernickel Bread	Brown Sugar Pecan Bread
22	33
Black Pumpernickel	Sally Lunn Bread
23	33
Beer Mustard Bread	Anadama Bread
25	34

BASIC WHITE BREAD

This is an all-purpose white bread. It is a good basic recipe with which you can try different brands of flour and yeast, as well as experiment with slight variations in the amounts of ingredients.

450 g (1 lb) LOAF	INGREDIENTS	675 g (1½ lb) LOAF	METHOD
125 ml (4 fl oz)	water	185 ml (6½ fl oz)	Put all ingredients in bread tin in order suggested by your bread machine instructions. Set for white bread, medium crust. Press Start.
60 ml (2 fl oz)	milk	90 ml (3 fl oz)	
1 tbsp	butter	1½ tbsp	
1 tbsp	sugar	1½ tbsp	
1 tsp	salt	1½ tsp	
500 g (1 lb 2 oz)	bread flour	750 g (1 lb 11 oz)	
2 tsp	yeast	1 tbsp	

HONEY WHEAT BREAD

This is a dense, slightly sweet bread with a high proportion of whole-wheat flour. It is good for toast or sandwiches.

450 g (1 lb) LOAF	INGREDIENTS	675 g (1½ lb) LOAF	METHOD
125 ml (4 fl oz)	milk	185 ml (6½ fl oz)	Put ingredients in bread tin in order suggested by your bread machine instructions. Set for whole-wheat bread, medium crust. Press Start.
60 ml (2 fl oz)	water	90 ml (3 fl oz)	
2 tbsp	butter	3 tbsp	
3 tbsp	sugar	4½ tbsp	
¼ tsp	salt	1 tsp	
365 g (13 oz)	whole-wheat flour	550 g (1 lb 4 oz)	
115 g (4 oz)	bread flour	165 g (6½ oz)	
2 tsp	yeast	1 tbsp	

EGG BREAD

*This is another all-purpose white bread, but the addition of egg gives it
a subtly richer flavour and texture than basic white bread.*

450 g (1 lb) LOAF	INGREDIENTS	675 g (1½ lb) LOAF	METHOD
1	egg	1 + 1 yolk	Put ingredients in bread tin in order suggested by your bread machine instructions. Set for white bread, medium crust. Press Start.
125 ml (4 fl oz)	milk	185 ml (6½ fl oz)	
1 tbsp	butter	1½ tbsp	
2 tbsp	sugar	3 tbsp	
1 tsp	salt	1½ tsp	
500 g (1 lb 2 oz)	bread flour	750 g (1 lb 11 oz)	
1½ tsp	yeast	2¼ tsp	

SOUR CREAM CORNMEAL BREAD

*This bread is specifically for toast. Untoasted, it is dry.
Thinly sliced, it makes excellent melba toast.*

450 g (1 lb) LOAF	INGREDIENTS	675 g (1½ lb) LOAF	METHOD
1	egg	1	Put ingredients in bread tin in order suggested by your bread machine instructions. Set for white bread, medium crust. Press Start.
2 tbsp	water	80 ml (3 fl oz)	
125 ml (4 fl oz)	sour cream	185 ml (6½ fl oz)	
2 tbsp	butter	3 tbsp	
1 tbsp	sugar	1½ tbsp	
½ tsp	salt	¾ tsp	
125 g (5 oz)	cornmeal	200 g (7 oz)	
365 g (13 oz)	bread flour	550 g (1 lb 4 oz)	
1½ tsp	yeast	2¼ tsp	

RIGHT Egg Bread

ONION DILL RYE BREAD

This is a strongly flavoured rye bread, good for meat sandwiches.

450 g (1 lb) LOAF	INGREDIENTS	675 g (1½ lb) LOAF	METHOD
175 ml (6 fl oz)	water	250 ml (9 fl oz)	Put ingredients in bread tin in order suggested by your bread machine instructions. Set for whole-wheat bread, medium crust. Press Start.
1 tbsp	vegetable oil	1½ tbsp	
1 tbsp	sugar	1½ tbsp	
1 tsp	salt	1½ tsp	
2 tsp	dried dill	1 tbsp	
2 tsp	dehydrated minced onion	1 tbsp	
2 tbsp	cornmeal	3 tbsp	
325 g (12 oz)	bread flour	500 g (1 lb 2 oz)	
165 g (6½ oz)	rye flour	270 g (10 oz)	
2 tsp	yeast	1 tbsp	

LIGHT RYE BREAD

This light rye bread, made with beer, is lighter in colour and texture than most rye breads. Mildly flavoured, it is good for sandwiches.

450 g (1 lb) LOAF	INGREDIENTS	675 g (1½ lb) LOAF	METHOD
185 ml (6½ fl oz)	flat beer	270 ml (10 fl oz)	Put ingredients in bread tin in order suggested by your bread machine instructions. Set for whole-wheat bread, medium crust. Press Start.
1 tbsp	vegetable oil	1½ tbsp	
1 tbsp	honey	1½ tbsp	
1 tsp	salt	1½ tsp	
1 tsp	caraway seeds	1½ tsp	
300 g (11 oz)	bread flour	425 g (15 oz)	
250 g (9 oz)	rye flour	365 g (13 oz)	
2 tsp	yeast	1 tbsp	

RIGHT Onion Dill Rye Bread

PUMPERNICKEL BREAD

This is an excellent bread for sandwiches or canapés.

450 g (1 lb) LOAF	INGREDIENTS	675 g (1½ lb) LOAF
185 ml (6 fl oz)	milk	270 ml (10 fl oz)
1 tbsp	vegetable oil	1½ tbsp
2 tbsp	molasses	3 tbsp
½ tsp	salt	¾ tsp
2 tbsp	unsweetened cocoa powder	3 tbsp
2 tsp	caraway seeds	1 tbsp
75 g (3 oz)	bread flour	115 g (4 oz)
250 g (9 oz)	rye flour	365 g (13 oz)
115 g (4 oz)	whole-wheat flour	165 g (6½ oz)
2 tbsp	cornmeal	3 tbsp
2 tsp	yeast	1 tbsp

METHOD

Put ingredients in bread tin in order suggested by your bread machine instructions. Set for whole-wheat bread, medium crust. Press Start.

Alternatively, to make baguettes, remove dough from bread machine after first kneading and punch down. Cut dough in two equal parts. Roll each part into a thick rope, about 20 cm (8 in) long for the 450 g (1 lb) recipe, about 25 cm (10 in) for the 675 g (1½ lb) recipe. Put baguettes on a baking sheet that has been sprinkled with cornmeal. Put in a warm place and cover loosely. Let rise until doubled in volume. Bake in a preheated 180°C/350°F/Gas 4 oven about 25 minutes, or until loaves are crusty and sound hollow.

BUTTERMILK PUMPERNICKEL BREAD

This is a dense, flavourful rye bread, good for sandwiches. The dough should be checked early in the kneading stage to see if more liquid or flour is needed.

450 g (1 lb) LOAF	INGREDIENTS	675 g (1½ lb) LOAF
125 ml (4 fl oz)	buttermilk	185 ml (6½ fl oz)
60 ml (2 fl oz)	water	90 ml (3 fl oz)
1 tbsp	vegetable oil	1½ tbsp
2 tbsp	molasses	3 tbsp
1½ tsp	caraway seeds	2¼ tsp
¼ tsp	baking soda	¼ tsp
1 tsp	salt	1½ tsp
365 g (13 oz)	bread flour	550 g (1 lb 4 oz)
165 g (6½ fl oz)	pumpernickel flour	270 g (10 oz)
1½ tsp	yeast	2¼ tsp

METHOD

Put ingredients in bread tin in order suggested by your bread machine instructions. Set for whole-wheat bread, medium crust. Press Start.

BLACK PUMPERNICKEL

This is a very dense, very flavourful bread, made with a coarse grind of pumpernickel flour. Although the texture is lightened somewhat by the addition of mashed potatoes, it is not a high riser. It is delicious with sweet butter alone, but is also good for sandwiches. Because the grinds of pumpernickel flours vary widely, all breads may not have the same result.

450 g (1 lb) LOAF	INGREDIENTS	675 g (1½ lb) LOAF
40 g (1½ oz)	cornmeal	60 g (2¼ oz)
60 ml (2 fl oz)	boiling water	90 ml (3 fl oz)
60 ml (2 fl oz)	very strong coffee	90 ml (3 fl oz)
125 ml (4 fl oz)	mashed potatoes	185 ml (6½ fl oz)
2 tbsp	powdered milk	3 tbsp
2 tbsp	vegetable oil	3 tbsp
3 tbsp	molasses	4½ tbsp
1 tbsp	unsweetened cocoa	1½ tbsp
1 tsp	salt	1½ tsp
1 tsp	caraway seeds	1½ tsp
150 g (6 oz)	pumpernickel flour	250 g (9 oz)
325 g (12 oz)	bread flour	500 g (1 lb 2oz)
1½ tsp	yeast	2¼ tsp

METHOD

Put cornmeal in bread tin and pour boiling water over it. Stir. Let cool 15 minutes. If the coffee is hot, add it immediately after stirring in the water. Otherwise, add it with the other ingredients. Put remaining ingredients in bread tin in order suggested by your bread machine instructions. Set for whole-wheat bread, medium crust. Press Start.

BEER MUSTARD BREAD

Although seasoned with mustard and thyme, this bread is more subtly flavoured than you might expect. It goes well with meats, whether as a dinner bread or sandwich bread.

450 g (1 lb) LOAF	INGREDIENTS	675 g (1½ lb) LOAF
185 ml (6½ fl oz)	flat beer	270 ml (10 fl oz)
2 tbsp	powdered milk	3 tbsp
1 tbsp	vegetable oil	1½ tbsp
1 tbsp	sugar	1½ tbsp
2 tbsp	Dijon-style mustard	3 tbsp
½ tsp	dried thyme	¾ tsp
1 tsp	salt	1½ tsp
500 g (1 lb 2 oz)	bread flour	750 g (1 lb 11 oz)
1½ tsp	yeast	2¼ tsp

METHOD

Place all ingredients in bread tin in order recommended by your bread machine instructions. Set machine for white bread, medium crust. Press Start.

POTATO BREAD

Mashed potatoes add subtle flavour and texture to white bread. Use this as you would use ordinary white bread. Potatoes seasoned with garlic or herbs add a nice flavour to the bread.

450 g (1 lb) LOAF	INGREDIENTS	675 g (1½ lb) LOAF
125 ml (4 fl oz)	mashed potatoes	185 ml (6½ fl oz)
100 ml (3½ fl oz)	potato water	175 ml (6 fl oz)
2 tbsp	vegetable oil	3 tbsp
1 tbsp	honey	1½ tbsp
1 tsp	salt	1½ tsp
500 g (1 lb 2 oz)	bread flour	750 g (1 lb 11 oz)
2 tsp	yeast	1 tbsp

METHOD

Put ingredients in bread tin in order suggested by your bread machine instructions. If you don't have the water the potatoes were boiled in, use plain water. Set for white bread, medium crust. Press Start.

The recipe is based on plain mashed potatoes – no milk, butter or salt. However, if you have leftover mashed potatoes with additions, just adjust the recipe slightly, for example by reducing the water by 1 tablespoon.

LEFT Beer Mustard Bread

GRAHAM BREAD

*Graham flour, a coarsely ground whole-wheat flour, gives this bread a
slightly chewy texture. Molasses subtly changes the flavour. It is good for
toast, grilled cheese sandwiches, or as a dinner bread.*

450 g (1 lb) LOAF	INGREDIENTS	675 g (1½ lb) LOAF
185 ml (6½ fl oz)	water	270 ml (10 fl oz)
1 tbsp	vegetable oil	1½ tbsp
2 tbsp	molasses	3 tbsp
½ tsp	salt	¾ tsp
250 g (9 oz)	bread flour	365 g (13 oz)
250 g (9 oz)	graham flour	365 g (13 oz)
1½ tsp	yeast	2¼ tsp

METHOD

Put ingredients in bread tin in order suggested by your
bread machine instructions. Set for whole-wheat bread,
medium crust. Press Start.

RYE BREAD

This is a basic rye bread, good for sandwiches or as a dinner bread. It can be baked in the bread machine or in the oven.

450 g (1 lb) LOAF	INGREDIENTS	675 g (1½ lb) LOAF
185 ml (6½ fl oz)	water	270 ml (10 fl oz)
1 tbsp	vegetable oil	1½ tbsp
4 tsp	molasses	2 tbsp
1 tsp	salt	1½ tsp
2 tsp	caraway seeds	1 tbsp
365 g (13 oz)	bread flour	550 g (1 lb 4 oz)
165 g (6½ oz)	rye flour	270 g (10 oz)
2 tsp	yeast	1 tbsp

METHOD

Put ingredients in bread tin in order suggested by your bread machine instructions. Set for whole-wheat bread, medium crust. Press Start.

For oven-baked bread, set machine for dough stage. When dough is ready, remove it from the machine and press down. Shape it into a large ball and flatten it slightly. Or roll it into a fat baguette. Place it on a baking sheet that has been sprinkled with cornmeal. Cover the bread loosely, set it in a warm place, and let it rise until doubled in volume, about 1 hour.

Make a wash of 1 egg lightly beaten with 1 tablespoon of milk. Gently brush the egg wash over the top and sides of the loaf. Bake the bread in a preheated 190°C/375°F/Gas 5 oven until top and bottom are crusty and sound hollow when thumped, about 35 minutes.

CORNMEAL YEAST BREAD

Boiled cornmeal adds flavour to this pale yellow bread. It's good for toast, sandwiches, or just eaten warm with sweet butter.

450 g (1 lb) LOAF	INGREDIENTS	675 g (1½ lb) LOAF
250 ml (9 fl oz)	water	375 ml (13 fl oz)
1 tsp	salt	1½ tsp
1½ tbsp	butter	2¼ tbsp
100 g (3½ oz)	cornmeal	125 g (5 oz)
60 ml (2 fl oz)	milk	90 ml (3 fl oz)
1 tsp	sugar	1½ tbsp
415 g (15½ oz)	bread flour	675 g (1½ lb)
1½ tsp	yeast	2¼ tsp

METHOD

Boil water in small saucepan. Add salt and butter. Then pour cornmeal in a thin stream constantly stirring, until mixture forms a thick paste. Cook one minute longer, stirring all the while. Remove mixture from heat and set aside to cool.

When cornmeal paste has cooled, put it in the bread tin along with the other ingredients in the order suggested by your bread machine instructions. Set for white bread, medium crust. Press Start.

BUTTERMILK OATMEAL BREAD

Oatmeal, wheat germ and buttermilk give this bread a soft, loose texture and delicate flavour. It is delicious with cheese.

450 g (1 lb) LOAF	INGREDIENTS	675 g (1½ lb) LOAF
80 ml (3 fl oz)	very hot water	125 ml (4 fl oz)
100 g (3½ oz)	rolled oats (not quick oatmeal)	125 g (5 oz)
145 ml (5 fl oz)	buttermilk	240 ml (8 fl oz)
1 tbsp	butter	1½ tbsp
2 tbsp	sugar	3 tbsp
1 tsp	salt	1½ tsp
½ tsp	baking soda	½ tsp
2 tbsp	wheat germ	3 tbsp
415 g (15½ oz)	bread flour	675 g (1½ lb)
1½ tsp	yeast	2¼ tsp

METHOD

Put oats in bread tin. Pour very hot or boiling water over the oats and stir. Let sit at least 15 minutes. Put remaining ingredients in bread tin in order suggested by your bread machine instructions. Set for white bread, medium crust. Press Start.

RIGHT Cornmeal Yeast Bread

ITALIAN HERB BREAD

This is a delicious white bread, seasoned with garlic and Italian herbs. It makes delicious cheese or meat sandwiches, and is an excellent dinner bread.

450 g (1 lb) LOAF	INGREDIENTS	675 g (1½ lb) LOAF
2 tbsp	olive oil	3 tbsp
1	clove garlic, pressed	1 or 2
1 tsp	dried basil	1½ tsp
½ tsp	dried oregano	¾ tsp
¼ tsp	dried rosemary	¼ tsp
¼ tsp	dried thyme	½ tsp
125 ml (4 fl oz)	water	185 ml (6½ fl oz)
60 ml (2 fl oz)	milk	90 ml (3 fl oz)
1 tsp	sugar	1½ tsp
1 tsp	salt	1½ tsp
500 g (1 lb 2 oz)	bread flour	750 g (1 lb 11 oz)
1½ tsp	yeast	2¼ tsp

METHOD

Heat oil in a small frying pan. Add the garlic and herbs. Saute for 2 minutes, taking care not to let the garlic scorch or it will turn bitter. If necessary, remove the pan from the stove. The herbs will continuing cooking in the oil's heat.

Put the herb oil and remaining ingredients in bread tin in order suggested by your bread machine instructions. Set for white bread, medium crust. Press Start.

ORANGE CUMIN BREAD

This light whole-wheat bread is slightly sweet, and is flavoured with orange and cumin, a pungent spice frequently used in Mexican, Middle Eastern, Asian and Mediterranean cooking. Try this bread with chicken or fish.

450 g (1 lb) LOAF	INGREDIENTS	675 g (1½ lb) LOAF
125 ml (4 fl oz)	milk	185 ml (6½ fl oz)
60 ml (2 fl oz)	water	90 ml (3 fl oz)
2 tbsp	vegetable oil	3 tbsp
3 tbsp	sugar	4½ tbsp
1 tbsp	grated orange peel	1½ tbsp
¼ tsp	ground cumin	1¼ tsp
1 tsp	salt	1½ tsp
2 tbsp	cornmeal	3 tbsp
365 g (13 oz)	bread flour	550 g (1 lb 4 oz)
115 g (4 oz)	whole-wheat flour	165 g (6½ oz)
1½ tsp	yeast	2¼ tsp

METHOD

Put ingredients in bread tin in order suggested by your bread machine instructions. Set for whole-wheat bread, medium crust. Press Start.

Brown Sugar Pecan Bread

This is a slightly sweet bread. Try it toasted with cream cheese.

450 g (1 lb) LOAF	INGREDIENTS	675 g (1½ lb) LOAF
125 ml (4 fl oz)	water	185 ml (6½ fl oz)
60 ml (2 fl oz)	milk	90 ml (3 fl oz)
2 tbsp	butter	3 tbsp
3 tbsp	brown sugar	4½ tbsp
1½ tsp	cinnamon	2¼ tsp
½ tsp	salt	¾ tsp
40 g (1½ oz)	oat bran	60 g (2¼ oz)
500 g (1 lb 2 oz)	bread flour	750 g (1 lb 11 oz)
1½ tsp	yeast	2¼ tsp
100 g (3½ oz)	chopped pecans	125 g (5 oz)

METHOD

Put all ingredients except pecans in bread tin in order suggested by your bread machine instructions. Set for white bread, medium crust. Press Start. Add pecans after first kneading or when machine beeps to add fruit or nuts.

Sally Lunn Bread

Sally Lunn bread originated in Great Britain, but the southern United States has claimed it as its own. Traditionally it is baked in a tube tin.

450 g (1 lb) LOAF	INGREDIENTS	675 g (1½ lb) LOAF
80 ml (3 fl oz)	milk	125 ml (4 fl oz)
2	eggs	3
50 g (2 oz)	butter	75 g (3 oz)
3 tbsp	sugar	4½ tbsp
½ tsp	salt	¾ tsp
500 g (1 lb 2 oz)	bread flour	750 g (1 lb 11 oz)
1½ tsp	yeast	2¼ tsp

METHOD

Put ingredients in bread tin in order suggested by your bread machine instructions. Set for sweet bread, light crust. Press Start.

Alternatively, to bake the bread in a tube tin in the oven, set bread machine for the dough stage. When ready, remove dough and punch it down. The larger loaf goes in a 12 cm (9 in) or 25.5 cm (10 in) tube tin. The small loaf will fit in a 15 cm (6 in) or 18 cm (7 in) tube tin or 1.5 l (53 fl oz) soufflé or casserole dish. Butter the tin and turn the dough in it so all sides are buttered. Cover loosely, put in a warm spot to rise until doubled in volume. Bake in a preheated 180°C/350°C/Gas 4 oven until golden and a skewer inserted in the bread comes out clean, 25 to 30 minutes.

LEFT Brown Sugar Pecan Bread

ANADAMA BREAD

Anadama bread is a New England hearth bread, made with cornmeal and molasses. For variety, substitute 150 g (6 oz) whole-wheat flour for an equal amount of the bread flour.

450 g (1 lb) LOAF	INGREDIENTS	675 g (1½ lb) LOAF
185 ml (6½ fl oz)	water	270 ml (10 fl oz)
1 tbsp	vegetable oil	1½ tbsp
3 tbsp	molasses	4½ tbsp
1 tsp	salt	1½ tsp
40 g (1½ oz)	cornmeal	60 g (2¼ oz)
500 g (1 lb 2 oz)	bread flour	750 g (1 lb 11 oz)
1½ tsp	yeast	2¼ tsp

METHOD

Put ingredients in bread tin in order suggested by your bread machine instructions. Set for white bread, medium crust. Press Start.

Grain Breads

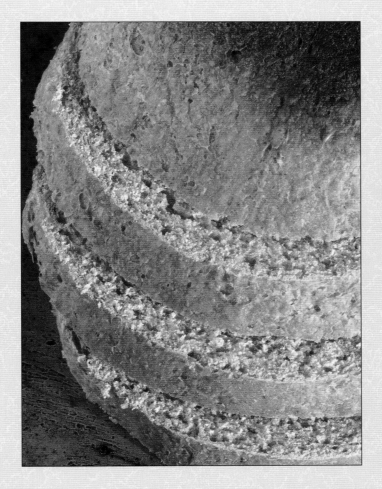

MULTI-GRAIN BREAD
36

BULGUR WHEAT BREAD
36

CRACKED WHEAT BUTTERMILK BREAD
37

SEED BREAD
39

MILLET BREAD
39

MAPLE PECAN BREAKFAST BREAD
40

PRUNE WALNUT BRAN BREAD
41

COCONUT BANANA BRAN BREAD
42

BRAN CEREAL BREAD
42

HONEY ORANGE MULTI-GRAIN BREAD
44

WHEAT GERM YOGURT BREAD
44

SUNSHINE BREAD
45

APPLE BRAN BREAD
47

MULTI-GRAIN BREAD

This is a densely textured bread with the flavour of several grains. It includes enough bread flour that it rises into a small, compact loaf.

450 g (1 lb) LOAF	INGREDIENTS	675 g (1½ lb) LOAF
125 ml (4 fl oz)	water	185 ml (6½ fl oz)
60 ml (2 fl oz)	milk	90 ml (3 fl oz)
2 tbsp	vegetable oil	3 tbsp
2 tbsp	honey	3 tbsp
1 tsp	salt	1½ tsp
40 g (1½ oz)	wheat germ	60 g (2¼ oz)
40 g (1½ oz)	oat bran	60 g (2¼ oz)
165 g (6½ oz)	bread flour	270 g (10 oz)
250 g (9 oz)	whole-wheat flour	365 g (13 oz)
2 tsp	yeast	1 tbsp

METHOD

Put ingredients in bread tin in order suggested by your bread machine instructions. Set for whole-wheat bread, medium crust. Press Start.

BULGUR WHEAT BREAD

Bulgur is cracked wheat that has been parboiled. It adds fibre and crunch to whole-wheat bread.

450 g (1 lb) LOAF	INGREDIENTS	675 g (1½ lb) LOAF
185 ml (6½ fl oz)	buttermilk	270 ml (10 fl oz)
2 tbsp	vegetable oil	3 tbsp
2 tbsp	honey	3 tbsp
1 tsp	salt	1½ tsp
¼ tsp	baking soda	¼ tsp
3 tbsp	bulgur	4½ tbsp
1 tbsp	cornmeal	1½ tbsp
250 g (9 oz)	bread flour	365 g (13 oz)
250 g (9 oz)	whole-wheat flour	365 g (13 oz)
2 tsp	yeast	1 tbsp

METHOD

Put ingredients in bread tin in order suggested by your bread machine instructions. Set for whole-wheat bread, medium crust. Press Start.

CRACKED WHEAT BUTTERMILK BREAD

*This is a moist, hearty whole-wheat bread, with cracked wheat adding
texture and heft. It is a good sandwich bread.*

450 g (1 lb) LOAF	INGREDIENTS	675 g (1½ lb) LOAF
40 g (1½ oz)	cracked wheat	60 g (2¼ oz)
130 ml (4½ fl oz)	buttermilk	200 ml (7 fl oz)
2 tbsp	butter	3 tbsp
2 tbsp	honey	3 tbsp
1 tsp	salt	1½ tsp
¼ tsp	baking soda	¼ tsp
250 g (9 oz)	bread flour	365 g (13 oz)
250 g (9 oz)	whole-wheat flour	365 g (13 oz)
2 tsp	yeast	1 tbsp

METHOD

Put cracked wheat in small saucepan with 1 to 2 cups
water. Bring to a boil, then reduce heat to medium and
let boil for 6 minutes. Remove from heat and drain
thoroughly. Let wheat cool about 15 minutes.

Put cooked wheat and all other ingredients in bread tin
in order suggested by your bread machine instructions.
Set for whole-wheat bread, medium crust. Press Start.
Check the dough after about 10 minutes of kneading.
Depending on how well-drained the cracked wheat was,
the bread may need a little more buttermilk or flour.

SEED BREAD

*Wheat germ, sesame seeds and sunflower seeds add crunch
to this light whole-wheat bread.*

450 g (1 lb) LOAF	INGREDIENTS	675 g (1½ lb) LOAF
125 ml (4 fl oz)	buttermilk	185 ml (6½ fl oz)
80 ml (3 fl oz)	water	125 ml (4 fl oz)
1 tbsp	vegetable oil	1½ tbsp
1 tbsp	sugar	1½ tbsp
¼ tsp	baking soda	¼ tsp
1 tsp	salt	1½ tsp
2 tbsp	toasted wheat germ	3 tbsp
115 g (4 oz)	whole-wheat flour	165 g (6½ oz)
365 g (13 oz)	bread flour	550 g (1 lb 4 oz)
1½ tsp	yeast	2¼ tsp
3 tbsp	raw, shelled sunflower seeds	4½ tbsp
1 tbsp	toasted sesame seeds	1½ tbsp

METHOD

Put all ingredients except seeds in bread tin in order suggested by your bread machine instructions. Set for whole-wheat bread, medium crust. Press Start. Add seeds after first kneading or when machine beeps to add nuts.

To toast wheat germs and sesame seeds, put each in a small, ungreased frying pan over medium heat. Shake the pan occasionally so seeds do not scorch. Cook until they are lightly brown. Let seeds or wheat germ cool before adding them to the dough.

MILLET BREAD

*This bread uses two forms of millet. The millet flour adds flavour, and whole
hulled millet gives it crunch. Use it for cheese on toast or for sandwiches.*

450 g (1 lb) LOAF	INGREDIENTS	675 g (1½ lb) LOAF
185 ml (6½ fl oz)	water	270 ml (10 fl oz)
1 tbsp	vegetable oil	1½ tbsp
2 tbsp	honey	3 tbsp
1 tsp	salt	1½ tsp
3 tbsp	whole hulled millet	4½ tbsp
75 g (3 oz)	millet flour	115 g (4 oz)
150 g (6 oz)	whole-wheat flour	250 g (9 oz)
250 g (9 oz)	bread flour	365 g (13 oz)
2 tsp	yeast	1 tbsp

METHOD

Put ingredients in bread tin in order suggested by your bread machine instructions. Set for whole-wheat bread, medium crust. Press Start.

LEFT Seed Bread

Maple Pecan Breakfast Bread

This multi-grain bread is sweetened with maple syrup but it is still not a sweet bread. Flavour also comes from pecans, which are added at the beginning and ground up by the kneading action. Bulgur wheat, softened slightly by boiling water, also adds texture.

450 g (1 lb) LOAF	INGREDIENTS	675 g (1½ lb) LOAF
40 g (1½ oz)	bulgur wheat	60 g (2¼ oz)
60 ml (2 fl oz)	boiling water	90 ml (3 fl oz)
125 ml (4 fl oz)	milk	185 ml (6½ fl oz)
2 tbsp	butter	3 tbsp
3 tbsp	maple syrup	4½ tbsp
1 tsp	salt	1½ tsp
40 g (1½ oz)	chopped pecans	60 g (2¼ oz)
40 g (1½ oz)	oat bran	60 g (2¼ oz)
165 g (6½ oz)	whole-wheat flour	270 g (10 oz)
250 g (9 oz)	bread flour	365 g (13 oz)
1½ tsp	yeast	2¼ tsp

METHOD

Put bulgur in bread tin. Pour boiling water over it and stir. Let cool 15 minutes. Put remaining ingredients in bread tin in order suggested by your bread machine instructions. Set for whole-wheat bread, medium crust. Press Start.

PRUNE WALNUT BRAN BREAD

This is a delicious bread, made moist and slightly sweet by prunes, and fortified with bran cereal. Even prune-haters like this bread, as long as they don't know prunes are the secret ingredient. The walnuts are added at the beginning, so they are ground up more finely than usual, adding more flavour than crunch.

450 g (1 lb) LOAF	INGREDIENTS	675 g (1½ lb) LOAF
175 ml (6 fl oz)	water	250 ml (9 fl oz)
3 tbsp	powdered milk	4½ tbsp
125 ml (4 fl oz)	chopped pitted prunes	185 ml (6½ fl oz)
1 tbsp	vegetable oil	1½ tbsp
1 tbsp	molasses	1½ tbsp
1 tsp	salt	1½ tsp
40 g (1½ oz)	chopped walnuts	60 g (2¼ oz)
100 g (3½ oz)	bran flakes (cereal)	125 g (5 oz)
250 g (9 oz)	whole-wheat flour	365 g (13 oz)
250 g (9 oz)	bread flour	365 g (13 oz)
1½ tsp	yeast	2¼ tsp

METHOD

Put ingredients in bread tin in order suggested by your bread machine instructions. Set for whole-wheat bread, medium crust. Press Start.

Coconut Banana Bran Bread

This is a dense, hearty bread, only slightly sweet but fragrant with tropical flavours. It makes excellent toast, but don't limit yourself to butter – spread it with cream cheese or peanut butter. Use a bran cereal such as All-Bran, not bran flakes.

450 g (1 lb) LOAF	INGREDIENTS	675 g (1½ lb) LOAF
1	egg	1
60 ml (2 fl oz)	milk	125 ml (4 fl oz)
80 ml (3 fl oz)	mashed ripe banana	125 ml (4 fl oz)
2 tbsp	butter	3 tbsp
2 tbsp	honey	3 tbsp
40 g (1½ oz)	flaked coconut	60 g (2¼ oz)
½ tsp	salt	¾ tsp
50 g (2 oz)	bran cereal	100 g (3½ oz)
250 g (9 oz)	whole-wheat flour	365 g (13 oz)
250 g (9 oz)	bread flour	365 g (13 oz)
1½ tsp	yeast	2¼ tsp

METHOD

Put ingredients in bread tin in order suggested by your bread machine instructions. Set for whole-wheat bread, medium crust. Press Start.

Bran Cereal Bread

This is a dense but moist bread, high in fibre provided by bran cereal (not flakes) such as All-Bran. It makes good bread for toast or sandwiches.

450 g (1 lb) LOAF	INGREDIENTS	675 g (1½ lb) LOAF
210 ml (7 fl oz)	milk	330 ml (12 fl oz)
1 tbsp	vegetable oil	1½ tbsp
1 tbsp	sugar	1½ tbsp
1 tsp	salt	1½ tsp
50 g (2 oz)	bran cereal	100 g (3½ oz)
165 g (6½ oz)	whole-wheat flour	270 g (10 oz)
250 g (9 oz)	bread flour	365 g (13 oz)
1½ tsp	yeast	2¼ tsp

METHOD

Put ingredients in bread tin in order suggested by your bread machine instructions. Set for whole-wheat bread, medium crust. Press Start.

RIGHT Coconut Banana Bran Bread

HONEY ORANGE MULTI-GRAIN BREAD

This bread, perfect for breakfast, is dense with a soft texture, moist and flavourful. Millet and bulgur wheat add a little crunch.

450 g (1 lb) LOAF	INGREDIENTS	675 g (1½ lb) LOAF
80 ml (3 fl oz)	water	125 ml (4 fl oz)
125 ml (4 fl oz)	buttermilk	185 ml (6½ fl oz)
1 tbsp	vegetable oil	1½ tbsp
2 tbsp	honey	3 tbsp
1 tbsp	grated orange rind	1½ tbsp
1 tsp	salt	1½ tsp
1 tbsp	bulgur wheat	1½ tbsp
1 tbsp	whole hulled wheat	1½ tbsp
40 g (1½ oz)	soya flour	60 g (2¼ oz)
40 g (1½ oz)	amaranth flour	60 g (2¼ oz)
150 g (6 oz)	whole-wheat flour	250 g (9 oz)
325 g (12 oz)	bread flour	500 g (1 lb 2 oz)
2 tsp	yeast	1 tbsp

METHOD

Put ingredients in bread tin in order suggested by your bread machine instructions. Set for whole-wheat bread, medium crust. Press Start.

WHEAT GERM YOGURT BREAD

This healthy bread has a dense but soft texture. It is good for toast or sandwiches.

450 g (1 lb) LOAF	INGREDIENTS	675 g (1½ lb) LOAF
125 ml (4 fl oz)	plain yogurt	185 ml (6½ fl oz)
60 ml (2 fl oz)	water	90 ml (3 fl oz)
1 tbsp	vegetable oil	1½ tbsp
2 tbsp	honey	3 tbsp
1 tsp	salt	1½ tsp
3 tbsp	powdered milk	4½ tbsp
40 g (1½ oz)	toasted wheat germ	60 g (2¼ oz)
250 g (9 oz)	bread flour	365 g (13 oz)
250 g (9 oz)	whole-wheat flour	365 g (13 oz)
2 tsp	yeast	1 tbsp

METHOD

Put ingredients in bread tin in order suggested by your bread machine instructions. Set for whole-wheat bread, medium crust. Press Start.

To toast wheat germ, put it in a small dry frying pan over medium heat. Cook, shaking occasionally so germ doesn't scorch, until lightly browned. Let wheat germ cool before adding to to the dough.

SUNSHINE BREAD

This is a light, whole-wheat bread from California, full of dates and sunflower seeds. It makes good toast and vegetarian-type sandwiches of avocado or cream cheese.

450 g (1 lb) LOAF	INGREDIENTS	675 g (1½ lb) LOAF
125 ml (4 fl oz)	sour cream	185 ml (6½ fl oz)
60 ml (2 fl oz)	water	90 ml (3 fl oz)
2 tbsp	butter	3 tbsp
2 tbsp	honey	3 tbsp
½ tsp	salt	¾ tsp
2 tbsp	oat bran	3 tbsp
115 g (4 oz)	whole-wheat flour	165 g (6½ oz)
365 g (13 oz)	bread flour	550 g (1 lb 4 oz)
1½ tsp	yeast	2¼ tsp
3 tbsp	sunflower seeds	4½ tbsp
40 g (1½ oz)	chopped dates	60 g (2¼ oz)

METHOD

Put all ingredients except sunflower seeds and dates in bread tin in order suggested by your bread machine instructions. Set for whole-wheat bread, medium crust. Press Start. Add seeds and dates at the beeper or after first kneading.

APPLE BRAN BREAD

This breakfast bread, fragrant with apple and cinnamon and enriched with wheat germ and bran cereal, makes excellent toast. As the water content of apples varies, you may need to add a small amount of water or flour. However, check the dough late in the kneading stage, as the bran flakes will absorb some liquid.

450 g (1 lb) LOAF	INGREDIENTS	675 g (1½ lb) LOAF
80 ml (3 fl oz)	peeled, grated apple	125 ml (4 fl oz)
125 ml (4 fl oz)	water	185 ml (6½ fl oz)
2 tbsp	butter	3 tbsp
2 tbsp	honey	3 tbsp
3 tbsp	powdered milk	4½ tbsp
1 tsp	salt	1½ tsp
1 tsp	cinnamon	1½ tsp
100 g (3½ oz)	bran flakes (cereal)	125 g (5 oz)
2 tbsp	toasted wheat germ	3 tbsp
250 g (9 oz)	whole-wheat flour	365 g (13 oz)
165 g (6½ oz)	bread flour	270 g (10 oz)
1½ tsp	yeast	2¼ tsp

METHOD

Put ingredients in bread tin in order suggested by your bread machine instructions. Set for whole-wheat bread, medium crust. Press Start.

To toast wheat germ, put it in a small, dry frying pan. Cook over medium heat until browned. Shake and stir frequently to keep wheat germ from scorching. Let it cool before adding to bread tin.

Fruit, Vegetable, Nut and Cheese Breads

Date Granola Bread	Tropical Pineapple Bread
49	59
Sweet Potato Bread	Cinnamon Raisin Bread
49	60
Zucchini Bread	Laura's Ginger Apple Sauce Bread
50	60
Cottage Cheese Dill Bread	Mango Macadamia Nut Bread
50	61
Chilli Cheese Bread	Trail Mix Bread
52	62
Basil Tomato Parmesan Bread	Apricot Graham Bread
53	62
Pumpkin Pecan Bread	Pear Bread
54	64
Cherry Hazelnut Bread	Cranberry Orange Bread
55	65
Olive Cheese Bread	Buttermilk Fruit Bread
56	66
Oatmeal Walnut Bread	Sweet Red Pepper Sage Bread
56	67
Apple Sauce Hazelnut Bread	California Almond Fig Bread
58	68
Ricotta Walnut Herb Bread	Almond Poppy Seed Bread
58	68

DATE GRANOLA BREAD

The variety of granolas available is tremendous. Different types can entirely change the character of the bread. Other than additions like dried fruits and nuts, the biggest difference is in sweetness. This bread, served untoasted with butter, was a favourite with the friends who tried many of my experiments.

450 g (1 lb) LOAF	INGREDIENTS	675 g (1½ lb) LOAF
125 ml (4 fl oz)	water	185 ml (6½ fl oz)
60 ml (2 fl oz)	milk	90 ml (3 fl oz)
1 tbsp	vegetable oil	1½ tbsp
1 tbsp	honey	1½ tbsp
½ tsp	cinnamon	¾ tsp
1 tsp	salt	1½ tsp
100 g (3½ oz)	granola	125 g (5 oz)
300 g (11 oz)	bread flour	425 g (15 oz)
115 g (4 oz)	whole-wheat flour	165 g (6½ oz)
1½ tsp	yeast	2¼ tsp
50 g (2 oz)	chopped dates	85 g (3 oz)

METHOD

Put all ingredients except dates in bread tin in order suggested by your bread machine instructions. Set for whole-wheat bread, medium crust. Press Start. Add dates after first kneading or when machine beeps to add fruit.

This recipe is based on a basic, not-too-sweet granola. You can adjust the amount of honey in the recipe if you're starting with a particularly sweet granola, substitute other fruit, or add nuts. Omit the cinnamon if the granola is already spiced.

SWEET POTATO BREAD

Sweet potato bread has its roots in the southern United States. It has a delicate flavour and pale orange colour, but is not a sweet bread. Serve it as an accompaniment to soup or salad, or top it with melted cheese.

450 g (1 lb) LOAF	INGREDIENTS	675 g (1½ lb) LOAF
175 ml (6 fl oz)	cooked, mashed sweet potatoes	250 ml (9 fl oz)
90 ml (3 fl oz)	milk	135 ml (4½ fl oz)
2 tbsp	butter	3 tbsp
2 tbsp	sugar	3 tbsp
1 tsp	salt	1½ tsp
500 g (1 lb 2 oz)	bread flour	750 g (1 lb 11 oz)
2 tsp	yeast	1 tbsp

METHOD

Put ingredients in bread tin in order suggested by your bread machine instructions. Set for whole-wheat bread, medium crust.

You may use canned sweet potatoes for this recipe, but only if there is no sugar or syrup added. Otherwise, bake or boil sweet potatoes and mash them without any additions. The amount of milk needed may vary slightly depending on the water content of the sweet potatoes.

Zucchini Bread

This is a medium-weight whole-wheat bread. Cottage cheese lightens it, bulgur wheat adds crunch, and zucchini (courgette) adds subtle flavour. It makes excellent toast, and is also good for sandwiches. The amount of water needed may vary, depending on the water content of the cottage cheese, so check the dough during kneading.

450 g (1 lb) LOAF	INGREDIENTS	675 g (1½ lb) LOAF
125 ml (4 fl oz)	cottage cheese	185 ml (6½ fl oz)
60 ml (2 fl oz)	water	90 ml (3 fl oz)
125 ml (4 fl oz)	grated raw courgettes	185 ml (6½ fl oz)
2 tbsp	butter	3 tbsp
1 tbsp	sugar	1½ tbsp
1 tsp	salt	1½ tsp
3 tbsp	bulgur wheat	4½ tbsp
150 g (6 oz)	whole-wheat flour	250 g (9 oz)
325 g (12 oz)	bread flour	500 g (1 lb 2 oz)
1½ tsp	yeast	2¼ tsp

METHOD

Put ingredients in bread tin in order suggested by your bread machine instructions. Set for whole wheat-bread, medium crust. Press Start.

Cottage Cheese Dill Bread

Cottage cheese gives this bread a feathery light texture. Try it in a sandwich. The amount of water needed may vary slightly, depending on the liquid content of the cottage cheese.

450 g (1 lb) LOAF	INGREDIENTS	675 g (1½ lb) LOAF
175 ml (6 fl oz)	cottage cheese	250 ml (9 fl oz)
1	egg	1 egg + 1 yolk
2½ tbsp	water	4 tbsp
1 tbsp	butter	1½ tbsp
1 tbsp	honey	1½ tbsp
½ tsp	salt	¾ tsp
365 g (13 oz)	bread flour	550 g (1 lb 4 oz)
115 g (4 oz)	whole-wheat flour	165 g (6½ oz)
2 tsp	dried dill	1 tbsp
1½ tsp	yeast	2¼ tsp

METHOD

Put ingredients in bread tin in order suggested by your bread machine instructions. Set for whole-wheat bread, medium crust. Press Start.

RIGHT Zucchini Bread

CHILLI CHEESE BREAD

This is a very flavourful bread, with the complementary tastes of Cheddar cheese and green chillies. If using fresh chillies, choose Anaheims, green New Mexico chillies or poblanos. You may add a jalapeno or two serrano chillies for extra heat. A note at the bottom of this recipe tells how to roast your own chillies, but you can substitute canned green chillies with a small loss of flavour. This is a hearty bread that goes well with soups, stews and salads.

450 g (1 lb) LOAF	INGREDIENTS	675 g (1½ lb) LOAF
2	roasted and chopped chillies	3
1	egg	1
80 ml (3 fl oz)	milk	135 ml (4½ fl oz)
175 g (6 oz)	grated sharp Cheddar cheese	250 g (9 oz)
2 tbsp	butter	3 tbsp
1 tsp	sugar	1½ tsp
1 tsp	salt	1½ tsp
500 g (1 lb 2 oz)	bread flour	750 g (1 lb 11 oz)
1½ tsp	yeast	2¼ tsp

METHOD

Put ingredients in bread tin in order suggested by your bread machine instructions. Set for white bread, medium crust. Press Start.

To roast chillies: set grill. Cut chillies in half lengthwise (poblanos should be cut in three or four lengthwise pieces). Remove stems and seeds, taking care to avoid handling the seeds or inner veins. Place skin side up on foil or grill pan 10 to 15 cm (4 to 6 in) under grill. Grill until the skin is blistered and mostly brown or black, but don't let the flesh burn. Don't expect the skin to cook uniformly. Remove chillies from grill and place in bag or foil envelope and close. Let the chillies steam in the foil or bag for about 10 minutes. Remove chillies from bag. Peel and discard skin. Chop chillies.

Basil Tomato Parmesan Bread

This is a moist and savoury bread, seasoned with basil, Parmesan cheese and sun-dried tomatoes. Serve it with sweet butter, or use it for sandwiches. You can add the tomatoes at the beginning or after the initial kneading. If you add the tomatoes at the same time as the other ingredients, the bread will be a deep red-orange with very few bits of tomato.

450 g (1 lb) LOAF	INGREDIENTS	675 g (1½ lb) LOAF
125 ml (4 fl oz)	water	185 ml (6½ fl oz)
60 ml (2 fl oz)	milk	90 ml (3 fl oz)
2 tbsp	olive oil	3 tbsp
1 tsp	sugar	1½ tsp
1 tsp	salt	1½ tsp
2 tsp	dried basil	3 tsp
80 ml (3 fl oz)	grated Parmesan cheese	125 ml (4 fl oz)
500 g (1 lb 2 oz)	bread flour	750 g (1 lb 11 oz)
2 tsp	yeast	1 tbsp
40 g (1½ oz)	chopped sun-dried tomatoes	60 g (2¼ oz)

METHOD

Add all ingredients except tomatoes in the order suggested by bread machine instructions. Set machine for white bread, medium crust. Press Start.

If tomatoes are oil-packed, blot them dry. (Tomato oil may be used instead of all or part of the olive oil in the recipe.) Chop tomatoes or cut with kitchen scissors. Add them to the dough after the first kneading, or when the beeper indicates it is time to add fruit.

PUMPKIN PECAN BREAD

This is not the traditional sweet, dense baking powder pumpkin bread, but a light and slightly sweet yeast bread that is flavoured with pumpkin, pecans and spices. Eat it warm with butter or make turkey sandwiches with it.

450 g (1 lb) LOAF	INGREDIENTS	675 g (1½ lb) LOAF
80 ml (3 fl oz)	milk	125 ml (4 fl oz)
185 ml (6½ fl oz)	puréed pumpkin	270 ml (10 fl oz)
2 tbsp	butter	3 tbsp
3 tbsp	sugar	4½ tbsp
½ tsp	salt	¾ tsp
1 tsp	cinnamon	1½ tsp
½ tsp	ground ginger	¾ tsp
¼ tsp	ground cloves	¼ tsp
100 g (3½ oz)	chopped pecans	125 g (5 oz)
500 g (1 lb 2 oz)	bread flour	750 g (1 lb 11 oz)
2 tsp	yeast	1 tbsp

METHOD

Put ingredients in bread tin in order suggested by your bread machine instructions. Set for white bread, light crust. Press Start.

The amount of milk needed may vary slightly, depending on the water content of the pumpkin. Be sure you are using pure pumpkin, not pumpkin pie filling.

CHERRY HAZELNUT BREAD

This is a light whole-wheat bread, made special by the addition of tart dried cherries and toasted hazelnuts. It is not a sweet bread, so it goes with meals.

450 g (1 lb) LOAF	INGREDIENTS	675 g (1½ lb) LOAF
125 ml (4 fl oz)	milk	200 ml (7½ fl oz)
1	egg	1
2 tbsp	butter	3 tbsp
2 tbsp	sugar	3 tbsp
½ tsp	salt	¾ tsp
365 g (13 oz)	bread flour	550 g (1 lb 4 oz)
115 g (4 oz)	whole-wheat flour	165 g (6½ oz)
1½ tsp	yeast	2¼ tsp
40 g (1½ oz)	dried cherries	60 g (2¼ oz)
3 tbsp	chopped toasted hazelnuts	4½ tbsp

METHOD

Put all ingredients except cherries and hazelnuts in bread tin in order suggested by your bread machine instructions. Set for whole-wheat bread, medium crust. Press Start. Add cherries and hazelnuts after the first kneading, or when the machine signals to add fruit.

Note: to toast shelled hazelnuts, spread them in a single layer on an ungreased baking sheet. Bake them in a 180°C/350°F/Gas 4 oven for 10 minutes, stirring two or three times. Allow the nuts to cool, wrap them in a coarse towel, and rub them together to remove the papery membrane.

OLIVE CHEESE BREAD

This is an assertive bread, flavoured with green olives, feta cheese, sun-dried tomatoes and thyme. Serve it with pasta, homemade tomato soup, antipasto, or salad. It can be baked in the bread machine, or shaped into a round loaf and baked in the oven.

450 g (1 lb) LOAF	INGREDIENTS	675 g (1½ lb) LOAF
175 ml (6 fl oz)	water	250 ml (9 fl oz)
2 tbsp	olive oil	3 tbsp
1 tbsp	sugar	1½ tbsp
½ tsp	dried thyme	¾ tsp
1 tsp	salt	1½ tsp
500 g (1 lb 2 oz)	bread flour	750 g (1 lb 11 oz)
1½ tsp	yeast	2¼ tsp
50 g (2 oz)	crumbled feta cheese	85 g (3 oz)
40 g (1½ oz)	coarsely chopped green olives	60 g (2¼ oz)
2 tbsp	chopped sun-dried tomatoes	3 tbsp
2 tbsp	bread flour	3 tbsp

METHOD

Put first seven ingredients in bread tin in order suggested by your bread machine instructions. Set for white bread, medium crust. Press Start. Toss remaining ingredients with flour, then add them to the dough after first kneading or at the beeper.

To bake in the oven, set the bread machine for dough stage. When dough is ready, remove and punch down. Shape into a round loaf. Put on a baking sheet that has been sprinkled with cornmeal. Cover loosely and put in a warm place to rise until doubled in volume. Brush the surface with a glaze of 1 egg mixed with 1 tbsp water, and bake in a preheated 180°C/350°F/Gas 4 oven until golden, about 25 minutes.

OATMEAL WALNUT BREAD

Old-fashioned rolled oats add a nice texture to this breakfast bread.

450 g (1 lb) LOAF	INGREDIENTS	675 g (1½ lb) LOAF
125 ml (4 fl oz)	milk	185 ml (6½ fl oz)
60 ml (2 fl oz)	water	90 ml (3 fl oz)
1 tbsp	butter	1½ tbsp
2 tbsp	honey	3 tbsp
1 tsp	salt	1½ tsp
415 g (15½ oz)	bread flour	675 g (1½ lb)
100 g (3½ oz)	rolled oats	125 g (5 oz)
100 g (3½ oz)	chopped walnuts	125 g (5 oz)
1½ tsp	yeast	2¼ tsp

METHOD

Put ingredients in bread tin in order suggested by your bread machine instructions. Set for white bread, medium crust. Press Start.

RIGHT Olive Cheese Bread

APPLE SAUCE HAZELNUT BREAD

This apple-flavoured bread is only slightly sweet but fragrant with spice.
Oatmeal and hazelnuts give it a nice texture. It is best as a breakfast bread.

450 g (1 lb) LOAF	INGREDIENTS	675 g (1½ lb) LOAF
100 g (3½ fl oz)	old-fashioned rolled oats	125 g (5 oz)
80 ml (3 fl oz)	boiling water	125 ml (4 fl oz)
80 ml (3 fl oz)	unsweetened apple sauce	125 ml (4 fl oz)
60 ml (2 fl oz)	water	90 ml (3 fl oz)
1 tbsp	vegetable oil	1½ tbsp
1 tbsp	honey	1½ tbsp
½ tsp	cinnamon	¾ tsp
¼ tsp	allspice	½ tsp
2 tbsp	powdered milk	3 tbsp
½ tsp	salt	¾ tsp
415 g (15½ oz)	bread flour	675 g (1½ lb)
1½ tsp	yeast	2¼ tsp
40 g (1½ oz)	chopped toasted hazelnuts	60 g (2¼ oz)

METHOD

Put oatmeal in bread tin. Pour boiling water over oatmeal. Stir and let sit 15 minutes. Add remaining ingredients, except hazelnuts, in order suggested by your bread machine instructions. Set for white bread, medium crust. Press Start. Add hazelnuts after first kneading or at beeper.

The apple sauce should be thick. If it is runny, simmer it in a small saucepan to evaporate excess water. Measure the apple sauce after cooking, since water may account for nearly half the volume of some shop-bought apple sauce. Also check the dough after five minutes of kneading and add water or flour if needed. Omit the honey if the apple sauce is pre-sweetened.

RICOTTA WALNUT HERB BREAD

Try this bread with meatloaf sandwiches, pasta, light soups and salads.

450 g (1 lb) LOAF	INGREDIENTS	675 g (1½ lb) LOAF
2 tbsp	olive oil	3 tbsp
1 tsp	dried basil	1½ tsp
175 ml (6 fl oz)	ricotta cheese	250 ml (9 fl oz)
1	egg	1 egg + 1 yolk
3 tbsp	milk	4½ tbsp
2 tsp	sugar	1 tbsp
1 tsp	salt	1½ tsp
500 g (1 lb 2 oz)	bread flour	750 g (1 lb 11 oz)
1½ tsp	yeast	2¼ tsp
40 g (1½ oz)	chopped walnuts	60 g (2¼ oz)

METHOD

Heat oil in a frying pan. Add basil. Cook for 1 minute over low heat. Remove from heat and let it cool.

Drain off any watery liquid from the ricotta cheese.

Put cooled basil oil, drained ricotta, and all remaining ingredients except walnuts in bread tin in order suggested by your bread machine instructions. Set for white bread, medium crust. Press Start. Add the walnuts at the beeper or after the first kneading.

TROPICAL PINEAPPLE BREAD

*Candied pineapple sweetens this bread, which is also flavoured with coconut,
nutmeg and ginger. It is delicious toasted and spread with cream cheese.*

450 g (1 lb) LOAF	INGREDIENTS	675 g (1½ lb) LOAF
125 ml (4 fl oz)	water	185 ml (6½ fl oz)
60 ml (2 fl oz)	milk	90 ml (3 fl oz)
2 tbsp	butter	3 tbsp
2 tbsp	honey	3 tbsp
¼ tsp	ground ginger	½ tsp
¼ tsp	nutmeg	½ tsp
½ tsp	salt	¾ tsp
115 g (4 oz)	whole-wheat flour	165 g (6½ oz)
365 g (13 oz)	bread flour	550 g (1 lb 4 oz)
1½ tsp	yeast	2¼ tsp
50 g (2 oz)	diced sugared pineapple	100 g (3½ oz)
40 g (1½ oz)	grated coconut	60 g (2¼ oz)
40 g (1½ oz)	chopped macadamia nuts	60 g (2¼ oz)

METHOD

Put all but last three ingredients in bread tin in order
suggested by your bread machine instructions. Add
about half the pineapple, which will be cut into bits by
the kneading. Set for white bread, medium crust. Press
Start. Add remaining pineapple, coconut and nuts at
beeper or after first kneading.

CINNAMON RAISIN BREAD

This is a light, slightly sweet whole-wheat bread. It is good for toast, and delicious with apple or pumpkin butter.

450 g (1 lb) LOAF	INGREDIENTS	675 g (1½ lb) LOAF
125ml (4 fl oz)	water	185 ml (6½ fl oz)
60 ml (2 fl oz)	milk	90 ml (3 fl oz)
2 tbsp	butter	3 tbsp
3 tbsp	brown sugar	4½ tbsp
½ tsp	salt	¾ tsp
2 tsp	cinnamon	1 tbsp
365 g (13 oz)	bread flour	550 g (1 lb 4 oz)
115 g (4 oz)	whole-wheat flour	165 g (6½ oz)
2 tsp	yeast	1 tbsp
50 g (2 oz)	raisins	85 g (3 oz)

METHOD

Put all ingredients except raisins in bread tin in order suggested by your bread machine instructions. Set for whole-wheat bread, medium crust. Press Start. Add raisins after the first kneading, or when the machine signals that it is time to add fruit.

If you want whole raisins, add them after the first kneading. Add them at the beginning if you want a darker colour and an overall sweeter, raisiny taste. If your raisins are so dry that you plump them up in hot water, blot every bit of water off them before adding them. Wet raisins will throw off the flour/ liquid balance.

LAURA'S GINGER APPLE SAUCE BREAD

The flavour of ginger and apples is just right in this bread, tasty but not overwhelming. Graham flour gives it good texture.

450 g (1 lb) LOAF	INGREDIENTS	675 g (1½ lb) LOAF
80 ml (3 fl oz)	water	125 ml (4 fl oz)
125 ml (4 fl oz)	unsweetened apple sauce	185 ml (6½ fl oz)
2 tbsp	powdered milk	3 tbsp
1 tbsp	butter	1½ tbsp
2 tbsp	molasses	3 tbsp
1 tsp	ground ginger	1½ tsp
½ tsp	salt	¾ tsp
250 g (9 oz)	bread flour	365 g (13 oz)
250 g (9 oz)	graham flour	365 g (13 oz)
1½ tsp	yeast	2¼ tsp

METHOD

Put ingredients in bread tin in order suggested by your bread machine instructions. Set for whole-wheat bread, medium crust. Press Start.

The amount of water needed will depend on the water content of the apple sauce. If the apple sauce is runny, simmer it on the stovetop to evaporate excess water. Check the dough during kneading to see if the amount of flour or water needs to be adjusted.

Mango Macadamia Nut Bread

With its tropical flavour, this bread goes well with a fruited chicken salad sandwich.

450 g (1 lb) LOAF	INGREDIENTS	675 g (1½ lb) LOAF
50 g (2 oz)	old-fashioned rolled oats	100 g (3½ oz)
60 ml (2 fl oz)	boiling water	90 ml (3 fl oz)
125 ml (4 fl oz)	puréed mango	185 ml (6½ fl oz)
60 ml (2 fl oz)	milk	90 ml (3 fl oz)
1 tbsp	butter	1½ tbsp
2 tsp	sugar	1 tbsp
½ tsp	salt	¾ tsp
¼ tsp	ground ginger	½ tsp
¼ tsp	nutmeg	½ tsp
415 g (15½ oz)	bread flour	675 g (1½ lb)
2 tsp	yeast	1 tbsp
40 g (1½ oz)	chopped macadamia nuts	60 g (2¼ oz)

METHOD

Put the oats in bread machine tin and pour the boiling water over them. Stir so all the oats are wet. Let sit at least 15 minutes. Add all the remaining ingredients except the nuts. Set for white bread, medium crust. Press Start. Check the dough after about 10 minutes. Depending on the water content of the mango, the dough may need a little more milk or flour. Add the nuts after the first kneading or when the machine signals to add fruit or nuts.

TRAIL MIX BREAD

Trail mix is a kitchen-sink sort of concoction made up of any kind of dried fruit, seeds or nuts, from the ordinary to the exotic, and may be sweetened with bits of coconut, or other goodies. Likewise, Trail Mix Bread is a kitchen-sink sort of bread.

450 g (1 lb) LOAF	INGREDIENTS	675 g (1½ lb) LOAF
125 ml (4 fl oz)	water	185 ml (6½ fl oz)
60 ml (2 fl oz)	milk	90 ml (3 fl oz)
2 tbsp	vegetable oil	3 tbsp
2 tbsp	honey	3 tbsp
1 tsp	salt	1½ tsp
325 g (12 oz)	bread flour	500 g (1 lb 2 oz)
150 g (6 oz)	whole-wheat flour	250 g (9 oz)
1½ tsp	yeast	2¼ tsp
100 g (3½ oz)	trail mix	125 g (5 oz)

METHOD

Put all ingredients except trail mix in bread tin in order suggested by your bread machine instructions. Set for whole-wheat bread, medium crust. Press Start. Add trail mix at the beeper or after first kneading.

If the only trail mix you can find is a mix of raisins and sunflower seeds, doctor it with dates, dried apricots, dried cherries, pecans or cashews. Coarsely chop whole nuts such as almonds. Avoid using chocolate in the trail mix as it tends to burn in a bread machine.

APRICOT GRAHAM BREAD

Dried apricots and molasses give this bread a hint of sweetness, while the graham flour gives it a slightly chewy texture. It's a delicious breakfast bread that also goes well with chicken or cream cheese sandwiches.

450 g (1 lb) LOAF	INGREDIENTS	675 g (1½ lb) LOAF
175 ml (6 fl oz)	water	250 ml (9 fl oz)
1 tbsp	vegetable oil	1½ tbsp
2 tbsp	molasses	3 tbsp
50 g (2 oz)	coarsely chopped dried apricots	85 g (3 oz)
2 tbsp	powdered milk	3 tbsp
½ tsp	salt	¾ tsp
250 g (9 oz)	bread flour	365 g (13 oz)
250 g (9 oz)	graham flour	365 g (13 oz)
1½ tsp	yeast	2¼ tsp

METHOD

Put ingredients in bread tin in order suggested by your bread machine instructions. Set for whole-wheat bread, medium crust. Press Start.

RIGHT Trail Mix Bread

PEAR BREAD

This is based on a bread made in the French countryside amid pear orchards.
It has a delicate, sweet flavour of pears. It is a nice tea or breakfast bread,
or can be used in mildly flavoured sandwiches such as cream
cheese and cucumber.

450 g (1 lb) LOAF	INGREDIENTS	675 g (1½ lb) LOAF
125 ml (4 fl oz)	pear purée	185 ml (6½ fl oz)
about 3 tbsp	pear liquid or water	4–5 tbsp
2 tsp	honey	1 tbsp
2 tbsp	butter	3 tbsp
½ tsp	salt	¼ tsp
½ tsp	ground ginger	¼ tsp
½ tsp	nutmeg	¼ tsp
500 g (1 lb 2 oz)	bread flour	750 g (1 lb 11oz)
1½ tsp	yeast	2¼ tsp

METHOD

Make the pear purée by peeling and coring 3 pears for
the smaller recipe, 4 or 5 pears for the larger one. Cut
each pear in several pieces and put in a small saucepan
with 1 or 2 tbsp water. Start cooking over very low heat.
The pears will quickly start releasing their own juices,
and no more water will be needed. Increase to medium
heat. Cook the pears until they are very soft, about 10
minutes. Then drain off as much liquid as you can,
saving the liquid. Put the pears in a blender or food
processor and purée.

Measure out the required amount of purée. Put it and
all other ingredients except pear liquid in bread tin in
order suggested by your bread machine instructions.
The amount of liquid needed for the bread will depend
on the liquid in the purée, so you'll need to watch the
dough for the first few minutes, adding pear liquid (or
plain water) until it reaches the proper consistency –
neither stiff nor too soft. Set for white bread, medium
crust. Press Start. Once you have added the liquid, the
bread does not need any further attention until it is
baked.

CRANBERRY ORANGE BREAD

This bread is flavoured with cranberries and orange peel, but don't save it only for the holidays. It is slightly sweet, but is not sweet enough to be a dessert bread. Use it for toast or sandwiches of turkey or pork.

450 g (1 lb) LOAF	INGREDIENTS	675 g (1½ lb) LOAF
125 ml (4 fl oz)	water	185 ml (6½ fl oz)
2 tbsp	butter	3 tbsp
3 tbsp	sugar	4½ tbsp
½ tsp	salt	¾ tsp
2 tsp	grated orange peel	1 tbsp
½ tsp	nutmeg	¾ tsp
175 ml (6 fl oz)	cranberries	250 ml (9 fl oz)
115 g (4 oz)	whole-wheat flour	165 g (6½ fl oz)
365 g (13 oz)	bread flour	550 g (1 lb 4 oz)
2 tsp	yeast	1 tbsp

METHOD

Put ingredients in bread tin in order suggested by your bread machine instructions. Set for white bread, medium crust. Press Start.

You may use fresh or frozen cranberries, but allow frozen cranberries to thaw before adding them to the dough. If you add whole cranberries at the same time as the other ingredients, the kneading action of the bread machine will chop them to the right size. Although the dough may initially seem dry, it will gain some liquid from the cranberries.

BUTTERMILK FRUIT BREAD

This is a light whole-wheat buttermilk bread with dried fruit and a pinch of cinnamon for flavour. Use any combination of dried fruit, including peaches, apricots, cherries, raisins and figs.

450 g (1 lb) LOAF	INGREDIENTS	675 g (1½ lb) LOAF
125 ml (4 fl oz)	buttermilk	210 ml (7 fl oz)
1	egg	1
2 tbsp	butter	3 tbsp
2 tbsp	sugar	3 tbsp
½ tsp	salt	¾ tsp
½ tsp	baking soda	½ tsp
½ tsp	cinnamon	¾ tsp
365 g (13 oz)	bread flour	550 g (1 lb 4 oz)
115 g (4 oz)	whole-wheat flour	165 g (6½ oz)
1½ tsp	yeast	2¼ tsp
50 g (2 oz)	coarsely chopped dried fruit	75 g (3 oz)

METHOD

Put all ingredients except fruit in bread tin in order suggested by your bread machine instructions. Set for whole-wheat bread, medium crust. Press Start. Add fruit after the first kneading or when the machine beeps that it's time to add fruit.

SWEET RED PEPPER SAGE BREAD

*Made with semolina flour, this is a very light bread. The sage, toasted
sesame seeds and roasted sweet red bell peppers make it very flavourful.*

450 g (1 lb) LOAF	INGREDIENTS	675 g (1½ lb) LOAF
125 ml (4 fl oz)	milk	185 ml (6½ fl oz)
80 ml (3 fl oz)	chopped, roasted sweet red peppers	125 ml (4 fl oz)
2 tbsp	olive oil	3 tbsp
1 tbsp	sugar	1½ tbsp
3 tbsp	toasted sesame seeds	4½ tbsp
1 tsp	salt	1½ tsp
½ tsp	dried sage	¾ tsp
325 g (12 oz)	bread flour	500 g (1 lb 2 oz)
150 g (6 oz)	semolina flour	250 g (9 oz)
1½ tsp	yeast	2¼ tsp

METHOD

Put ingredients in bread tin in order suggested by your
bread machine instructions. Set for white bread,
medium crust. Press Start

To toast sesame seeds: put seeds in a small, dry frying
pan over medium heat. Stir or shake the pan frequently
to stop seeds scorching. Let seeds cool before using.

To roast sweet red bell peppers: cut each pepper into 3
or 4 nearly flat pieces. Place on grill pan or doubled
sheet of aluminium foil. Cook under the grill until skin
turns black and blisters. The pieces won't cook evenly;
remove each piece when it is done. As you remove
each piece, put it in a bag or foil envelope to steam for
10 minutes, then peel off skin.

If you add the peppers at the beginning of the kneading,
in combination with yellow semolina flour they will
turn the bread orange. They will also release more
moisture into the bread. If you add the peppers late in
the kneading, you may need to add another tablespoon
of milk. You may use bottled roasted red peppers or
roast your own.

CALIFORNIA ALMOND FIG BREAD

The additions to this yogurt bread – almonds and figs – come from California's Central Valley. It is not a sweet bread, although the figs give it a hint of sweetness.

450 g (1 lb) LOAF	INGREDIENTS	675 g (1½ lb) LOAF
125 ml (4 fl oz)	plain yogurt	185 ml (6½ fl oz)
60 ml (2 fl oz)	water	90 ml (3 fl oz)
1 tbsp	vegetable oil	1½ tbsp
2 tbsp	honey	3 tbsp
½ tsp	salt	¾ tsp
3 tbsp	oat bran	4½ tbsp
500 g (1 lb 2 oz)	bread flour	750 g (1 lb 11 oz)
1½ tsp	yeast	2¼ tsp
50 g (2 oz)	coarsely chopped figs	85 g (3 oz)
3 tbsp	slivered blanched almonds	4½ tbsp

METHOD

Put all ingredients except figs and almonds in bread tin in order suggested by your bread machine instructions. Set for white bread, medium crust. Press Start. Add figs and almonds after the first kneading, or when the machine signals that it is time to add fruit.

ALMOND POPPY SEED BREAD

This is a light, barely sweet bread, with oatmeal adding texture. It is a good bread for breakfast or a snack, and not at all like those gummy, overly sweet muffins.

450 g (1 lb) LOAF	INGREDIENTS	675 g (1½ lb) LOAF
1	egg	1
125 ml (4 fl oz)	milk	200 ml (7 fl oz)
2 tbsp	butter	3 tbsp
2 tbsp	sugar	3 tbsp
1 tsp	almond extract	1½ tsp
2 tbsp	poppy seeds	3 tbsp
½ tsp	salt	¾ tsp
50 g (2 oz)	old-fashioned rolled oats	85 g (3 oz)
415 g (15½ oz)	bread flour	675 g (1½ lb)
1½ tsp	yeast	2¼ tsp
40 g (1½ oz)	slivered almonds	60 g (2¼ oz)

METHOD

Put all ingredients except almonds in bread tin in order suggested by your bread machine instructions. Set for white bread, medium crust. Press Start. Add almonds at the beeper or after the first kneading.

Oven-Baked Breads, Rolls, Breadsticks and Bagels

LEMON POPPY SEED PLAIT

Slightly sweet, flavoured with lemon and full of poppy seeds, this plaited bread makes an impressive appearance at brunch or tea.

450 g (1 lb) LOAF	INGREDIENTS	675 g (1½ lb) LOAF
1	egg	1 egg + 1 yolk
125 ml (4 fl oz)	lemon yogurt	185 ml (6½ fl oz)
3 tbsp	butter	4½ tbsp
3 tbsp	sugar	4½ tbsp
3 tbsp	poppy seeds	4½ tbsp
2 tsp	grated lemon peel	1 tbsp
1 tsp	salt	1½ tsp
500 g (1 lb 2 oz)	bread flour	750 g (1 lb 11 oz)
1½ tsp	yeast	2¼ tsp

GLAZE

1 egg white beaten with 2 tsp water

METHOD

Put all dough ingredients in bread machine tin. Set for white or sweet bread, dough stage. Press Start.

When dough is ready, remove from tin and punch down. Cut into three equal pieces. Let it rest 5 minutes. Butter a baking sheet. Roll each piece of dough into a rope, about 36.5 cm (14 in) for smaller loaf, 46 to 51 cm (18 to 20 in) for larger loaf. Plait three ropes together and tuck ends under. Cover dough and put in a warm place to rise until doubled, 45 minutes to 1 hour.

Brush dough with egg-water wash. Bake bread in a preheated 180°C/350°F/Gas 4 oven until golden, 25 to 30 minutes.

CROISSANTS

This is a much simplified version of the flaky layered croissant that requires so much time and patience to make. It is very buttery, but the butter is kneaded into the dough with the other ingredients instead of being folded in afterwards. It's very important that the butter is at room temperature – not melted – when it is used.

MAKES 16	INGREDIENTS	MAKES 24
125 ml (4 fl oz)	water	185 g (6½ fl oz)
2 tbsp	powdered milk	3 tbsp
115 g (4 oz)	butter	165 g (6½ oz)
1 tbsp	sugar	1½ tbsp
1 tsp	salt	1½ tsp
500 g (1 lb 2 oz)	bread flour	750 g (1 lb 11 oz)
2 tsp	yeast	1 tbsp

GLAZE

1 egg
pinch of salt

METHOD

Put all ingredients except glaze in bread tin in order suggested by your bread machine instructions. Set for white bread, dough stage. Press Start.

Lightly butter two baking sheets.

When dough is ready, remove from bread machine and punch down. Cut the smaller recipe in two pieces, the larger recipe into three pieces. Let dough rest 5 minutes. Roll each piece of dough into a circle about 25 cm (10 in) in diameter and 3 mm (⅛ in) thick. To get the dough this thin, you may need to let it relax a little during the rolling.

Cut each circle into eight equal wedges. Take each wedge and roll it one more time with the rolling pin to flatten it. Starting at the wide end of the wedge, roll up the dough toward the point, stretching the dough slightly as you go. Place, with tip under the roll, on baking sheet. Pull ends towards front so the roll forms a crescent.

Make glaze by beating egg and salt together with a fork. Brush croissants with glaze. Cover loosely and set in a warm place to rise until doubled, about 1 hour. Brush again with glaze. Bake in a preheated 190°C/375°F/Gas 6 oven until golden brown, 20 to 25 minutes.

GARLIC HERB MONKEY BREAD

This savoury pull-apart bread is a variation on the traditional sweet monkey bread. Small balls of garlic-flavoured dough are dipped in melted butter seasoned with garlic and herbs, and layered in a baking pan. Unlike sweet monkey bread, which tastes good hot or cold, garlic-herb monkey bread loses its charm when cold, so time the making of the bread to make sure it comes out of the oven 5 minutes before meal time.

450 g (1 lb) LOAF	INGREDIENTS	675 g (1½ lb) LOAF
185 ml (6½ fl oz)	milk	250 ml (9 fl oz)
2 tbsp	vegetable oil	3 tbsp
1 tsp	sugar	1½ tsp
1 tsp	salt	1½ tsp
1	clove garlic, pressed	1 or 2 small
365 g (13 oz)	bread flour	550 g (1 lb 4 oz)
115 g (4 oz)	whole-wheat flour	165 g (6½ oz)
1½ tsp	yeast	2¼ tsp
4 tbsp	butter	6 tbsp
2	cloves garlic, pressed	3
¼ tsp	dried sage	¼ tsp
¼ tsp	dried rosemary, crushed	¼ tsp
½ tsp	dried basil	¾ tsp

METHOD

Put first eight ingredients in bread tin in order suggested by your bread machine instructions. Set for whole-wheat bread, dough stage. Press Start.

A few minutes before dough is ready, melt butter in small frying pan. Add garlic and herbs. Sauté for 2 minutes. If the garlic or herbs brown too quickly, remove the pan from the heat and let the mixture continue cooking in its own heat. The garlic will give the bread a bitter flavour if it burns. Lightly oil baking dish.

Remove the dough from the bread machine and punch down. Roll dough into a thick log and cut out into 20 to 24 pieces for the small loaf, 30 to 36 pieces for the large loaf. Roll pieces of dough into balls (they do not need to be perfectly round). Dip each ball in butter-herb mixture and layer in baking tin. The pieces in the first layer should be close but not touching to give them room to rise. On each succeeding layer, place balls so they overlap empty spaces on the layer beneath. Drizzle any remaining butter over the dough in the tin.

Cover dough loosely and put it in a warm place to rise. When bread has doubled in volume, about 30 to 40 minutes, put it in preheated 180°C/350°F/Gas 4 oven. Bake until bread is lightly browned and a skewer inserted comes out clean, about 25 to 30 minutes. Invert bread on serving plate, remove baking pan, and serve.

If you need more time to coincide the baking with serving a meal, you can slow down the rising by putting the assembled bread in the refrigerator, then letting it return to room temperature before baking. Monkey bread is traditionally baked in a tube tin, 25 cm (10 in) across for the larger loaf, a 18 to 20 cm (7 or 8 in) tin for the smaller loaf. However, it looks impressive and tastes just as good when baked in round casserole dishes, about 2.5 cm (1 in) smaller in diameter than the tube tins.

CRISP BREADSTICKS

These thin bread sticks will keep for several days if they are stored in an airtight container.

MAKES 24	INGREDIENTS	MAKES 36
175 ml (6 fl oz)	water	250 ml (9 fl oz)
60 ml (2 fl oz)	vegetable oil	90 ml (3 fl oz)
2 tsp	sugar	1 tbsp
1 tsp	salt	1½ tsp
500 g (1 lb 2 oz)	bread flour	750 g (1 lb 11 oz)
2 tsp	yeast	1 tbsp
about 2 tbsp	vegetable oil	about 3 tbsp
1	egg white	1
2 tbsp	water	2 tbsp

sesame or poppy seeds or coarse salt, optional

METHOD

Put all but last three ingredients in bread tin in order suggested by your bread machine instructions. Set for white bread, dough stage. Press Start.

Grease 2 or 3 baking sheets.

When dough is ready, remove from bread tin and punch down. Cut smaller batch into 24 pieces, larger batch into 36 pieces. Roll each piece between your palms to from a very skinny rope, about 20 cm (8 in) long. Place bread sticks 2.5 cm (1 in) apart on baking sheets. Brush lightly with oil. Cover loosely and set in a warm place to rise 20 to 25 minutes.

Preheat oven to 180°C/350°F/Gas 4. Make wash of egg white and 2 tbsp water. Brush egg wash lightly on bread sticks. Sprinkle with seeds or salt, if desired. Bake until golden brown, about 25 minutes.

SOFT BREADSTICKS

These soft bread sticks do not keep well, but they are delicious still warm from the oven. Sprinkle them with sesame or poppy seeds or coarse salt.

MAKES 20	INGREDIENTS	MAKES 30
175 ml (9 fl oz)	water	250 ml (9 fl oz)
1	egg, separated	1
2 tbsp	vegetable oil	3 tbsp
2 tsp	sugar	1 tbsp
1 tsp	salt	1½ tsp
500 g (1 lb 2 oz)	bread flour	750 g (1 lb 11 oz)
1½ tsp	yeast	2¼ tsp
2 tbsp	water	2 tbsp

sesame or poppy seeds or coarse salt, optional

METHOD

Separate the egg and put the yolk in the bread tin. Save the white for glaze. Put remaining ingredients except last 2 tbsp water and seeds in bread tin in order suggested by your bread machine instructions. Set for white bread, dough stage. Press Start.

Grease 2 or 3 baking sheets. Make a wash of the egg white and 2 tbsp water. Preheat oven to 180°C/350°F/Gas 4.

When dough is ready, remove from bread machine and punch down. Cut the dough into 20 pieces for the smaller recipe, 30 pieces for the larger recipe. Roll each piece between your palms to form a rope about 15 cm (6 in) long. Place breadsticks on baking sheet about 4 cm (1½ in) apart. Brush with egg wash. Sprinkle with seeds or salt, if desired.

Bake breadsticks until golden, 20 to 25 minutes.

HAMBURGER BUNS AND HOT DOG ROLLS

Baking your own hamburger buns or hot dog rolls is as easy as making simple dinner rolls.

MAKES 6	INGREDIENTS	MAKES 9
1	egg	1
125 ml (4 fl oz)	milk	210 ml (7½ fl oz)
3 tbsp	butter	4½ tbsp
2 tbsp	sugar	3 tbsp
½ tsp	salt	¾ tsp
500 g (1 lb 2 oz)	bread flour	750 g (1 lb 11 oz)
2 tsp	yeast	1 tbsp
2 tbsp	milk	3 tbsp

sesame seeds, optional

METHOD

Put all ingredients except 2 or 3 tbsp milk and sesame seeds in bread tin in order suggested by your bread machine instructions. Set for white bread, dough stage. Press Start.

When dough is ready, remove from bread machine and punch down. Cut smaller recipe into 6 equal pieces, the larger recipe into 9 pieces. Let dough rest 5 minutes while you butter one or two baking sheets. For hamburger buns, roll each piece into a ball and flatten it to form a patty about 7.5 cm (3 in) wide and 1 cm (½ in) thick. For hot dog buns, roll each piece into a 15 cm (6 in) rope and flatten to 1 cm (½ in) thickness. Place rolls on baking sheet. Cover loosely and set in a warm place to rise 20 minutes. Preheat oven to 200°C/400°F/Gas 6.

Lightly brush tops of rolls with milk and sprinkle with sesame seeds, if desired. Bake to 12 to 15 minutes, until a skewer inserted in roll comes out clean.

RYE CRESCENT ROLLS

These rye dinner rolls add an elegant touch to any meal, casual or formal. They're so good that they don't need butter.

MAKES 16	INGREDIENTS	MAKES 24
175 ml (6 fl oz)	flat beer	250 g (9 fl oz)
2 tbsp	vegetable oil	3 tbsp
1 tbsp	honey	1½ tbsp
1 tsp	salt	1½ tsp
1 tsp	caraway seeds	1½ tsp
365 g (13 oz)	bread flour	550 g (1 lb 4 oz)
165 g (6½ oz)	rye flour	250 g (9 oz)
2 tsp	yeast	1 tbsp
2 tbsp	melted butter	3 tbsp

METHOD

Put all ingredients except melted butter in bread tin in order suggested by your bread machine instructions. Set for whole-wheat bread, dough stage. Press Start.

When dough is ready, remove it from the bread machine and punch it down. Cut the smaller recipe into two equal parts, the larger recipe into three parts. Let the dough rest for five minutes. Oil two or three baking sheets.

On a lightly floured surface, roll out the first section of dough into a circle 20 to 23 cm (8 to 9 in) in diameter. Cut the circle into eight wedges. Starting from the outside of the circle and working toward the point, loosely roll up each wedge. Stretch each roll slightly and pull it into a curve. Set it on the baking sheet with the point underneath. Repeat with all the wedges, then with the remaining dough.

Let the dough rise until doubled, about 1 hour. Brush rolls with melted butter. Bake in a preheated 200°C/400°F/Gas 6 oven until rolls are lightly browned, 12 to 15 minutes.

LEFT Rye Crescent Rolls

SEMOLINA BREAD

Semolina is a hard winter wheat or durum flour used to make pasta, but it also makes a good bread when mixed with other flours. By itself, it makes a very heavy, dense bread. However, this loaf, great with pasta, is light and flavourful.

450 g (1 lb) LOAF	INGREDIENTS	675 g (1½ lb) LOAF
185 ml (6½ fl oz)	water	250 ml (9 fl oz)
1 tsp	sugar	1½ tsp
1 tsp	salt	1½ tsp
365 g (13 oz)	bread flour	550 g (1 lb 4 oz)
150 g (6 oz)	semolina flour	250 g (9 oz)
1½ tsp	yeast	2¼ tsp

GLAZE

1 egg yolk beaten with 1 tsp water
2–3 tbsp sesame seeds

METHOD

Put all dough ingredients in bread machine tin. Set for white bread, dough stage. Press Start.

When dough is ready, remove from pan and punch down. Shape it into a fat baguette. Set it on a baking sheet that has been sprinkled with cornmeal. Cover dough and put in a warm place to rise until doubled, about 45 minutes.

Brush loaf with egg glaze and sprinkle with sesame seeds. Bake bread in preheated 190°C/375°F/Gas 5 oven until golden and bread sounds hollow when rapped on the bottom, about 30 minutes.

PESTO SWIRL BREAD

A delicious layer of pesto is spread on a light whole-wheat dough, rolled up and baked into a tasty loaf that goes well with soups, salads, pastas, and grilled meat and fish. You can use store-bought pesto or make your own, following the recipe below. It's important that you drain off excess oil from the pesto, but it can be added to the bread instead of plain oil.

450 g (1 lb) LOAF	INGREDIENTS	675 g (1½ lb) LOAF
125 ml (4 fl oz)	water	185 ml (6½ fl oz)
60 ml (2 fl oz)	milk	90 ml (3 fl oz)
1 tbsp	vegetable oil	1½ tbsp
1 tbsp	sugar	1½ tbsp
1 tsp	salt	1½ tsp
365 g (13 oz)	bread flour	550 g (1 lb 4 oz)
115 g (4 oz)	whole-wheat flour	165 g (6½ oz)
2 tsp	yeast	1 tbsp
60 ml (2 fl oz)	pesto	6 tbsp

METHOD

Put all ingredients except pesto in bread tin in order suggested by your bread machine instructions. Set for whole-wheat bread, dough stage. Press Start.

Butter a 24 cm (9½ in) loaf pan (large enough for either recipe).

Remove dough from bread machine and punch down. Let it rest 5 minutes. Roll it out on a lightly floured surface to form a rectangle about 20 cm (8 in) wide and 36.5 to 46 cm (14 to 18 in) long. Spread pesto evenly over surface. Roll the dough into a fat, 20 cm (8 in) cylinder. Tucking the edge under, put it in the loaf tin. Loosely cover and put in a warm place to rise for 1 hour.

Bake the loaf in a preheated 180°C/350°F/Gas 4 oven until top is golden and a skewer inserted in the bread comes out clean, 30 to 35 minutes. Remove the bread from the tin and put it on a wire rack to cool for at least 15 minutes.

PESTO

INGREDIENTS	METHOD
200 g (7 oz) fresh basil leaves	Put all ingredients except olive oil in blender. Blend, adding a little oil at a time. Keep the pesto rough and fairly dry so that oil doesn't soak into the dough.
2 tbsp walnut pieces	
1 clove garlic, peeled	
50 g (2 oz) Parmesan cheese	
pinch salt	
about 2 tbsp olive oil	

WHOLE-WHEAT POTATO CLOVERLEAF ROLLS

These light whole-wheat rolls are excellent with dinner. If desired, add ½ tsp dried oregano or dill, or 2 tsp fresh snipped chives.

MAKES 12-16	INGREDIENTS	MAKES 18-24
125 ml (4 fl oz)	mashed potatoes	185 ml (6½ fl oz)
1	egg	1
60 ml (2 fl oz)	milk	125 ml (4 fl oz)
1 tbsp	vegetable oil	1½ tbsp
1 tbsp	sugar	1½ tbsp
1 tsp	salt	1½ tsp
325 g (12 oz)	bread flour	500 g (1 lb 2 oz)
150 g (6 oz)	whole-wheat flour	250 g (9 oz)
2 tsp	yeast	1 tbsp
about 3 tbsp	melted butter	about 4 tbsp

METHOD

Put all ingredients except melted butter in bread tin in order suggested by your bread machine instructions. Set for whole-wheat bread, dough stage. Press Start.

Lightly oil 12 to 16 muffin cups for the smaller recipe, 18 to 24 muffin cups for the larger recipe.

When dough is ready, remove from bread machine and punch down. Cut smaller recipe into 12 to 16 equal pieces, the larger recipe into 18 to 24 pieces. Cut each piece into thirds. Roll each piece into a tiny ball and dip in the melted butter. Place three tiny balls in each muffin cup. Cover loosely and set in a warm place to rise until doubled, 45 minutes to 1 hour.

Preheat oven to 190°/375°F/Gas 4. Lightly brush tops of rolls with remaining melted butter. Bake 15 to 20 minutes, until tops are golden brown.

PUMPERNICKEL RAISIN ROLLS

*Soft and slightly sweet pumpernickel raisin rolls
are delicious with dinner.*

MAKES 8-12	INGREDIENTS	MAKES 12-16
1	egg	1
125 ml (4 fl oz)	milk	200 ml (7 fl oz)
3 tbsp	vegetable oil	4½ tbsp
2 tbsp	molasses	3 tbsp
½ tsp	salt	¾ tsp
2 tbsp	unsweetened cocoa powder	3 tbsp
1 tsp	caraway seeds	1½ tsp
165 g (6½ oz)	bread flour	270 g (10 oz)
165 g (6½ oz)	whole-wheat flour	270 g (10 oz)
165 g (6½ oz)	rye flour	270 g (10 oz)
2 tsp	yeast	1 tbsp
3 tbsp	raisins	4½ tbsp
1 tbsp	melted butter	1½ tbsp

METHOD

Put all ingredients except raisins in bread tin in order
suggested by your bread machine instructions. Set for
whole-wheat bread, dough stage. Press Start. Add the
raisins after the first kneading or when the machine
signals it's time to add fruit.

Lightly oil a 20 cm (8 in) or 23 cm (9 in) square pan
for the smaller recipe, a 23 × 33 cm (9 × 13 in) tin for
the larger recipe.

When dough is ready, remove from bread machine and
punch down. Cut smaller recipe into 8 to 12 equal
pieces, the larger recipe into 12 to 16 pieces. Roll each
piece into a ball – it does not have to be perfectly
round. Place balls about 1 cm (½ in) apart in baking tin.
Cover loosely and set in a warm place to rise until
doubled, about 1 hour.

Preheat oven to 200°C/400°F/Gas 6. Lightly brush tops
of rolls with melted butter. Bake 12 to 15 minutes, until
a skewer inserted in roll comes out clean.

FRENCH BREAD

*This recipe produces wonderful baguettes when
still warm, but will become stale within a day.*

450 g (1 lb) LOAF	INGREDIENTS	675 g (1½ lb) LOAF
185 ml (6½ fl oz)	water	250 ml (9 fl oz)
1 tsp	salt	1½ tsp
500 g (1 lb 2 oz)	bread flour	750 g (1 lb 11 oz)
2 tsp	yeast	1 tbsp

METHOD

Put ingredients in bread tin in order suggested by your
bread machine instructions. Set for French bread,
medium crust.

To make baguettes, remove dough from bread machine
after first kneading and punch down. Cut into two
equal pieces. On a lightly floured surface, roll each
piece into a thick rope, about 20 cm (8 in) long for the
450 g (1 lb) loaf, and 25 cm (10 in) for the larger loaf.
Place on a baking sheet that has been sprinkled with
cornmeal. With a sharp knife, cut several diagonal
slashes in the top of each loaf. Put dough in a warm
place, cover loosely, and let rise until doubled in
volume, 45 minutes to 1 hour. Make a wash of 1 tbsp
egg white plus 1 tbsp water. Lightly brush wash over
surface of loaves. Bake baguettes in preheated
200°C/400°F/Gas 6 oven for about 25 minutes, until
crust is golden brown and bread makes a hollow sound
when thumped on the bottom and the top.

For crustier bread, place a shallow pan of boiling water
on the bottom shelf of the oven. Or lightly spray water
from a spray bottle into the oven when baking begins,
and one or two more times during baking.

RIGHT Pumpernickel Raisin Rolls

GARLIC PEPPER POTATO ROLLS

These light dinner rolls are seasoned with garlic and black pepper, and will complement almost any entrée.

MAKES 8-12	INGREDIENTS	MAKES 12-16
1	egg	1 + 1 yolk
3 tbsp	milk	4½ tbsp
125 ml (4 fl oz)	mashed potatoes	185 ml (6½ fl oz)
2 tbsp	vegetable oil	3 tbsp
1 tbsp	sugar	1½ tbsp
2	cloves garlic, minced	3
1½ tsp	fresh-ground black pepper	2¼ tsp
1 tsp	salt	1½ tsp
500 g (1 lb 2 oz)	bread flour	750 g (1 lb 11 oz)
1½ tsp	yeast	2¼ tsp
2 tbsp	milk	3 tbsp

METHOD

Put all ingredients except milk in bread tin in order suggested by your bread machine instructions. Set for white bread, dough stage. Press Start.

Lightly oil a 20 cm (8 in) or 23 cm (9 in) square tin for the smaller recipe, a 23 × 33 cm (9 × 13 in) tin for the larger recipe.

When dough is ready, remove from bread machine and punch down. Cut smaller recipe into 8 to 12 equal pieces, the larger recipe into 12 to 16 pieces. Roll each piece into a ball – it does not have to be perfectly round. Place balls about 1 cm (½ in) apart in baking tin. Cover loosely and set in a warm place to rise until doubled, 45 minutes to 1 hour.

Preheat oven to 190°C/375°F/Gas 5. Lightly brush tops of rolls with milk. Bake 12 to 15 minutes, until rolls are golden and a skewer inserted in roll comes out clean.

ENGLISH MUFFINS

These English muffins are a bit crisper than the soft, store-bought kind, but they have a fresher flavour. The easiest way to make them is with a 7.5 cm (3 in) biscuit cutter and a griddle, but you can use a clean tuna or pineapple can and a large frying pan.

MAKES 10-12	INGREDIENTS	MAKES 15-18
60 ml (2 fl oz)	water	90 ml (3 fl oz)
½ tbsp	baking soda	¼ tsp
125 ml (4 fl oz)	milk	185 ml (6½ fl oz)
2 tbsp	vegetable oil	3 tbsp
2 tsp	sugar	1 tbsp
½ tsp	salt	¼ tsp
500 g (1 lb 2 oz)	bread flour	750 g (1 lb 11 oz)
2 tsp	yeast	1 tbsp
	cornmeal	

METHOD

Dissolve the baking soda in the water. Put the water and remaining ingredients except cornmeal in bread tin in order suggested by your bread machine instructions. Set for white bread, dough stage. Press Start.

Sprinkle cornmeal on a baking sheet or large platter. White cornmeal is more aesthetically pleasing on English muffins, but yellow will do the job just fine. When dough is ready, remove it and punch it down and cut it in half. Let it rest 5 minutes. Then on a lightly floured surface, roll out the first half to 4 mm (⅜ in) thick. With the biscuit cutter, cut out 7.5 cm (3 in) rounds. Put the rounds on the cornmeal-covered baking sheet, then turn to coat both sides. Repeat with the second half. If you wish, you may roll up the scraps, knead them a little, let the dough rest a few minutes, then roll it out and cut a few more muffins. Don't reroll yet again – the muffins will be tough.

Cover muffins and let them rise 45 minutes.

If you have a griddle, set it for moderate heat. If not, place a frying pan – preferably one with a non-stick finish – over moderate heat. If the griddle or pan is well-seasoned, it will not require oil. If not, use just the barest trace of oil to cook. Cook until muffin bottoms are nicely browned, then turn and cook the other side. Cooking time will vary according to the temperature of your stove from 6 to 10 minutes per side.

BAGELS

Dense and chewy, bagels are a delight when they are split and toasted and served with butter or cream cheese. They also make delicious sandwiches. You can experiment by adding chopped sautéed onions, or raisins and cinnamon, to the dough.

MAKES 8-10	INGREDIENTS	MAKES 12-15
1	egg	1
125 ml (4 fl oz)	milk	200 ml (7½ fl oz)
1 tbsp	vegetable oil	1½ tbsp
2 tsp	sugar	1 tbsp
½ tsp	salt	¾ tsp
500 g (1 lb 2 oz)	bread flour	750 g (1 lb 11 oz)
2 tsp	yeast	1 tbsp
1 tbsp	sugar	1 tbsp
1	egg white	1
2 tsp	water	2 tsp

sesame or poppy seeds or coarse salt

METHOD

Put all but last four ingredients in bread tin in order suggested by your bread machine instructions. Set for white bread, dough stage. Press Start.

When dough is ready, remove from bread machine and punch down. Cut smaller recipe into 8 to 10 equal pieces, the larger recipe into 12 to 15 pieces. Roll each piece between your palms to form a thin rope, about 20 cm (8 in) long with tapered ends. Bring ends together to form a circle, with the tapered ends overlapping. With moistened fingers, pinch or lightly knead the joined ends so the circle is securely fastened, or it will come apart later.

Set the bagels in a warm place to rise and cover them loosely. They should rise for 15 minutes. Preheat oven to 200°C/400°F/Gas 6. While they are rising, bring about 1.3 l (46 fl oz) of water to boil in a saucepan. Add 1 tbsp sugar. When the bagels have risen for 15 minutes, drop one or two at a time into the boiling water, handling them as gently as possible so they do not deflate. They will rise to the surface of the water and swell up. Let them cook 1 minute, then turn them over and let them cook 3 minutes longer.

Remove bagels, let drain over the water, and place on an ungreased baking sheet. Beat egg white with water and brush over bagels. Sprinkle with sesame or poppy seeds or coarse salt. Bake until golden, 20 to 25 minutes.

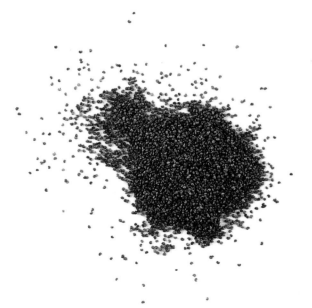

BREADS FROM AROUND THE WORLD

SWEDISH LIMPA BREAD

*This is a a slightly sweet rye bread, flavoured with a delicious combination
of orange peel, anise seed and caraway seed. It can be used for sandwiches
or canapés, but I like it best with only sweet butter.*

450 g (1 lb) LOAF	INGREDIENTS	675 g (1½ lb) LOAF
185 ml (6½ fl oz)	water	270 ml (10 fl oz)
1 tbsp	vegetable oil	1½ tbsp
2 tbsp	honey	3 tbsp
1 tsp	salt	1½ tsp
½ tsp	anise seed	¾ tsp
½ tsp	caraway seeds	¾ tsp
1 tbsp	grated orange peel	1½ tbsp
365 g (13 oz)	bread flour	550 g (1 lb 4 oz)
165 g (6½ oz)	rye flour	270 g (10 oz)
1½ tsp	yeast	2¼ tsp

METHOD

Put ingredients in bread tin in order suggested by your
bread machine instructions. Set for whole-wheat bread,
medium crust. Press Start.

PULLA

*Pulla is a Finnish sweet bread seasoned with cardamom, a spice widely used
in Scandinavian cooking. It is an everyday bread in Finland, often dressed up
with raisins and candied orange peel for holiday celebrations.*

450 g (1 lb) LOAF	INGREDIENTS	675 g (1½ lb) LOAF
1	egg	1 + 1 yolk
125 ml (4 fl oz)	milk	185 (6½ fl oz)
2 tbsp	butter	3 tbsp
3 tbsp	sugar	4½ tbsp
½ tsp	salt	¾ tsp
1 tsp	ground cardamom	1½ tsp
500 g (1 lb 2 oz)	bread flour	750 g (1 lb 11 oz)
2 tsp	yeast	1 tbsp

GLAZE

1 egg white beaten with 2 tsp water
2 tbsp sliced or slivered almonds
1–2 tbsp sugar

METHOD

Put all dough ingredients in bread machine tin. Set for
white or sweet bread, dough stage. Press Start.

When dough is ready, take out and punch down. Cut
into three equal pieces. Let it rest 5 minutes. Butter a
baking sheet. Roll each piece into a rope, about 40 cm
(16 in) for smaller loaf, 50 cm (20 in) for larger loaf.
Plait the ropes, tucking ends under. Cover dough and
put in a warm place to rise until doubled.

Brush dough with egg-water wash. Sprinkle with
almonds and then with sugar. Bake bread in preheated
190°C/375°F/Gas 5 oven until golden, about 35 minutes.

VERTERKAKE

This dense, sweet Norwegian bread takes its name from verterol, one of the ingredients in a Norwegian non-alcoholic beer. You can use alcoholic or non-alcoholic beer. This bread, adapted from a James Beard recipe, produces a soft dough that does not cook evenly in the bread machine, so it is baked in a conventional oven.

450 g (1 lb) LOAF	INGREDIENTS	675 g (1½ lb) LOAF
125 ml (4 fl oz)	flat dark beer	185 ml (6½ fl oz)
80 ml (3 fl oz)	milk	125 ml (4 fl oz)
2 tbsp	corn syrup	3 tbsp
2 tbsp	sugar	3 tbsp
¼ tsp	ground cloves	½ tsp
¼ tsp	black pepper	½ tsp
½ tsp	salt	¾ tsp
300 g (11 oz)	bread flour	450 g (1 lb)
250 g (9 oz)	rye flour	365 g (13 oz)
1½ tsp	yeast	2¼ tsp
2 tbsp	raisins	3 tbsp

METHOD

Put all ingredients except raisins in bread tin in order suggested by your bread machine instructions. Set for whole-wheat bread, dough stage. Press Start. Add raisins after first kneading or when the machine beeps that it is time to add fruit.

Oil a 21.5 to 24 cm (8½ to 9½ in) bread tin for the smaller loaf, a 24 to 26.5 cm (9½ to 10½ in) tin for the larger loaf.

When dough is ready, remove it from the bread machine and punch down. Shape it into a loaf. Place it in the bread tin, then turn so all sides of the dough are oiled. Cover loosely, set it in a warm place, and let it rise until doubled in bulk, 45 minutes to 1 hour.

Brush loaf with hot water and lightly prick the surface with a toothpick. Bake bread in a preheated 190°C/375°F/Gas 5 oven until loaf browns and sounds hollow when thumped, 35 to 45 minutes.

MOROCCAN BREAD

This is a heavy, coarsely textured bread, fragrant with anise. It is traditionally eaten with tagine, or Moroccan stew.

450 g (1 lb) LOAF	INGREDIENTS	675 g (1½ lb) LOAF
185 ml (6½ fl oz)	water	270 ml (10 fl oz)
¼ tsp	sugar	½ tsp
1½ tsp	anise seed	2¼ tsp
1 tsp	coarse salt	1½ tsp
115 g (4 oz)	whole-wheat flour	165 g (6½ oz)
365 g (13 oz)	bread flour	550 g (1 lb 4 oz)
2 tsp	yeast	1 tbsp

METHOD

Put all dough ingredients in bread machine tin. Set for whole-wheat bread, dough stage. Press Start.

When dough is ready, remove from tin and punch down. Shape it into a round loaf and place it on a baking sheet that has been sprinkled with cornmeal. Cover dough and put in a warm place to rise until doubled, 1 to 1½ hours.

Prick dough with a fork. Bake 12 minutes in a preheated 200°/400°F/Gas 6 oven, then reduce heat to 150°C/300°F/Gas 2 and bake about 40 minutes longer, until top and bottom sound hollow when rapped with your knuckles.

BATH BUNS

Bath buns, named after the English city where they originated, are made of a sweet egg dough, flavoured with mace and currants.

450 g (1 lb) LOAF	INGREDIENTS	675 g (1½ lb) LOAF
1	egg	1 + 1 yolk
125 ml (4 fl oz)	milk	185 ml (6½ fl oz)
50 g (2 oz)	butter	85 g (3 oz)
40 g (1½ oz)	sugar	60 g (2¼ oz)
¼ tsp	ground ginger	½ tsp
¼ tsp	mace	½ tsp
½ tsp	salt	¾ tsp
500 g (1 lb 2 oz)	bread flour	750 g (1 lb 11 oz)
2 tsp	yeast	1 tbsp
50 g (2 oz)	currants (or raisins)	100 g (3½ oz)

GLAZE

1 egg
1 tbsp milk
1–2 tbsp sugar

METHOD

Put all dough ingredients except currants in bread tin in order suggested by your bread machine instructions. Set for white or sweet bread, dough stage. Press Start. Add the currants after the first kneading or when the machine signals it's time to add fruit.

Butter a baking sheet. When dough is ready, remove from bread machine and punch down. Cut smaller recipe into 8 pieces, the larger recipe into 12. Roll each piece into a ball. Place balls on baking sheet and slightly flatten each one. Cover loosely and set in a warm place to rise until doubled, about 45 minutes.

Preheat oven to 200°C/400°F/Gas 6. Make glaze by fork-beating egg and milk. Lightly brush tops of rolls with glaze and sprinkle with sugar. Bake until buns are golden brown, 15 to 20 minutes.

RIGHT Bath Buns

PORTUGUESE SWEET BREAD

This is an eggy, light-textured sweet bread, flavoured with vanilla, lemon and nutmeg. It used to be eaten as an Easter bread in Portugal, but now is eaten as a breakfast bread year-round.

450 g (1 lb) LOAF	INGREDIENTS	675 g (1½ lb) LOAF
2	eggs	3
80 ml (3 fl oz)	milk	125 ml (4 fl oz)
2 tbsp	butter	3 tbsp
3 tbsp	sugar	4½ tbsp
½ tsp	salt	¾ tsp
1 tsp	vanilla	1½ tsp
2 tsp	grated lemon peel	1 tbsp
½ tsp	nutmeg	¾ tsp
500 g (1 lb 2 oz)	bread flour	750 g (1 lb 11 oz)
1½ tsp	yeast	2¼ tsp

METHOD

Put ingredients in bread tin in order suggested by your bread machine instructions. Set for white or sweet bread, light crust. Press Start.

FOCCACIO

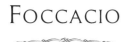

Serve wedges of this hearty bread as an hors d'oeuvre or with a meal instead of garlic bread. Instead of butter, dip pieces in high-quality olive oil. This bread is best served warm.

450 g (1 lb) LOAF	INGREDIENTS	675 g (1½ lb) LOAF
175 ml (6 fl oz)	water	250 ml (9 fl oz)
2 tbsp	olive oil	3 tbsp
1 tsp	salt	1½ tsp
500 g (1 lb 2 oz)	bread flour	750 g (1 lb 11 oz)
1¼ tsp	yeast	2 tsp
1 or 2	minced garlic cloves	2 or 3
1 tsp	dried rosemary	1½ tsp
1 tsp	coarse salt	1½ tsp
2 tbsp	olive oil	3 tbsp
2 tsp	grated Parmesan	1 tbsp

METHOD

Put first five ingredients in bread tin in order suggested by your bread machine instructions. Set for white bread, dough stage. Press Start.

Preheat oven to 200°C/400°F/Gas 6. Lightly sprinkle cornmeal on a baking sheet.

Remove dough and punch down. Let dough rest about 5 minutes. On a lightly floured surface, roll dough into a round, about 1 cm (½ in) thick. Place dough on baking sheet. Sprinkle the garlic, minced rosemary and coarse salt over the top, then lightly press it into the dough. With your fingertips, poke shallow indentations all over the top of the round. Pour the remaining olive oil over the top, letting it pool in the indentations. Sprinkle Parmesan over the top.

Bake bread until lightly browned, about 20 minutes.

BOLILLOS

These Mexican rolls are large and crusty, excellent with dinner.

450 g (1 lb) LOAF	INGREDIENTS	675 g (1½ lb) LOAF
175 ml (6 fl oz)	water	250 ml (6 fl oz)
1 tsp	sugar	1½ tsp
1 tsp	salt	1½ tsp
500 g (1 lb 2 oz)	bread flour	750 g (1 lb 11 oz)
1½ tsp	yeast	2¼ tsp

GLAZE

1 egg
1 tbsp water

METHOD

Put all ingredients except glaze in bread tin in order suggested by your bread machine instructions. Set for white bread, dough stage. Press Start.

Lightly oil a baking sheet.

When dough is ready, remove from bread machine and punch down. Cut smaller recipe into 6 equal pieces, the larger recipe into 9 pieces. Roll each piece into a ball. Flatten ball, then gently stretch and elongate to form an oval. Now, working on the long sides of the oval, fold those sides in toward the middle. Roll and stretch so the centre is thick and the ends are tapered like a spindle. Place the rolls, seam side down, on the baking sheet. Cover loosely and set in a warm place to rise until doubled, about 1 hour.

Preheat oven to 200°C/400°F/Gas 6. Lightly brush rolls with egg glaze. With a sharp knife or razor blade, make two diagonal slashes in the top of each roll. Bake 15 to 20 minutes, until rolls are golden and crusty.

PITTA BREAD

*These rounds of dough puff up when they are baked at high temperature. Cut
open an edge to create pockets that can be stuffed with all kinds of fillings.*

450 g (1 lb) LOAF	INGREDIENTS	675 g (1½ lb) LOAF
185 ml (6½ fl oz)	water	270 ml (10 fl oz)
1 tbsp	olive oil	1½ tbsp
1 tsp	sugar	1½ tsp
1 tsp	salt	1½ tsp
325 g (12 oz)	bread flour	500 g (1 lb 2 oz)
150 g (6 oz)	whole-wheat flour	250 g (9 oz)
1½ tsp	yeast	2¼ tsp

METHOD

Put ingredients in bread tin in order suggested by your
bread machine instructions and set for whole-wheat,
dough stage.

Punch down dough and cut into 6 equal pieces for
450 g (1 lb) recipe, 9 pieces for 675 g (1½ lb). Roll each
piece between your hands to form a ball. Flatten slightly

and let dough rest about 10 minutes. This will let the
dough relax so it will stretch more readily when you
roll it out, rather than bouncing back. On a lightly
floured surface, roll out each circle of dough to a
diameter of about 15 cm (6 in). Use flour sparingly,
as too much flour will interfere with the moisture
that creates steam and causes the dough to puff up.
Cover the dough with plastic wrap or a barely damp
towel, and let the dough rise about 30 minutes, until
it is puffy.

Preheat oven to 240°C/475°F/Gas 9. Lightly sprinkle
cornmeal on a baking sheet. When dough is ready,
carefully transfer rounds to the baking sheet. Bake until
dough puffs up and is lightly browned, 5 to 6 minutes,
then turn and bake until other side is lightly browned,
about 2 minutes.

BRIOCHE

*This buttery bread is not quite the same as the classic French brioche baked
in a fluted pan, but is a deliciously close cousin. Although it makes good
sandwiches, it is best served simply, toasted or untoasted, with butter.*

450 g (1 lb) LOAF	INGREDIENTS	675 g (1½ lb) LOAF
60 ml (2 fl oz)	water	90 ml (3 fl oz)
2	eggs	3
75 g (3 oz)	butter	115 g (4 oz)
1 tbsp	sugar	1½ tbsp
½ tsp	salt	¼ tsp
500 g (1 lb 2 oz)	bread flour	750 g (1 lb 11 oz)
1½ tsp	yeast	2¼ tsp

METHOD

Put ingredients in bread tin in order suggested by your
bread machine instructions. It is crucial that the butter
is softened to room temperature – not melted – when it
is added to the other ingredients. Set for white bread,
medium crust. Press Start.

PISTOLET

Pistolets are split rolls made in France and Belgium. Traditionally the dough is allowed to rise for several hours on the first rising to develop the flavour, then rise twice more. The dough is shaped into a plum-sized ball, then nearly split with the handle of a wooden spoon.

450 g (1 lb) LOAF	INGREDIENTS	675 g (1½ lb) LOAF
185 ml (6½ fl oz)	water	270 ml (10 fl oz)
3 tbsp	powdered milk	4½ tbsp
2 tbsp	butter	3 tbsp
1 tbsp	sugar	1½ tbsp
1 tsp	salt	1½ tsp
500 g (1 lb 2 oz)	bread flour	750 g (1 lb 11 oz)
1½ tsp	yeast	2¼ tsp
50 g (2 oz)	rye flour	85 g (3 oz)

METHOD

Put all ingredients except rye flour in bread tin in order suggested by your bread machine instructions. Set for white bread, dough stage. Press Start.

If your machine does not punch down the dough for you at this point, or if you can stop the machine, remove the pan. Cover it loosely, put it in a warm place and let dough continue rising for another two hours. It will have tripled in volume, and yeast flavours will have developed.

Punch the dough down and let it rise again for 45 minutes. Butter a baking sheet.

When dough is ready, punch it down. Cut smaller recipe into about 15 equal pieces, the larger recipe into about 22 pieces. Roll each piece into a ball. Dust the top with rye flour. Oil the dowel-like wooden handle of a large spoon. Use the handle to split each ball almost in half. The two sides of the ball should still be connected by a narrow strip of dough. Hold each pistolet at either end of the split with your thumbs in the trough. Pull gently to elongate the roll, and the sides will almost come together.

Traditionally, the roll is placed top (seam-side) down on the baking sheet. After it has risen, it is turned upright and baked. However, if you are all thumbs and tend to deflate the dough when you handle it, just leave it upright and let it rise with the seam side up. Cover them up loosely, put in a warm place, and let them rise for 30 minutes.

Preheat oven to 220°C/425°F/Gas 7. Pour boiling water into a shallow baking pan and place it on the bottom shelf of the oven. The steam will give the pistolets a crusty finish. Bake pistolets until they are golden brown and crusty, 15 to 20 minutes.

LAVOSH (ARMENIAN FLATBREAD)

Lavosh is a puffy flatbread that is crisper than pitta bread, but softer than a cracker. Rounds of lavosh are broken into pieces, not cut. Eat lavosh plain or with butter.

450 g (1 lb) LOAF	INGREDIENTS	675 g (1½ lb) LOAF
185 ml (6½ fl oz)	water	270 ml (10 fl oz)
3 tbsp	butter	4½ tbsp
1 tsp	salt	1½ tsp
500 g (1 lb 2 oz)	bread flour	750 g (1 lb 11 oz)
1½ tsp	yeast	2¼ tsp
1	egg	1
2 tbsp	water	3 tbsp
1–2 tsp	sesame or poppy seeds	2–3 tsp

METHOD

Put water, butter, salt, flour and yeast in bread tin in order suggested by your bread machine instructions. Set for white bread, dough stage.

Remove dough and punch down. Cut into 4 pieces for smaller recipe, 6 pieces for larger recipe. Roll each piece between your hands to form a ball, then flatten each ball slightly. Let dough relax for 10 minutes or so. This will help the dough stretch when you roll it out. Otherwise, it will keep bouncing back to its original shape.

Preheat oven to 200°C/400°F/Gas 6. Make a wash by lightly beating egg with remaining water.

On a lightly floured surface, roll out the first round of dough until it is paper thin. Transfer to a greased baking sheet. Working quickly, brush it with the egg wash. Sprinkle with seeds. Put the first round in the oven immediately, and repeat the process with each round. Bake the lavosh until it is puffy and lightly browned, 8 to 12 minutes.

Sourdough Breads

SOURDOUGH STARTER

Sourdough is the product of fermentation in dough that has been allowed to sit out for days and gather wild yeasts from the air. In ancient times, it was the only leavening known to bread bakers, and much effort was made to disguise its sour taste. It came back into common usage in mining camps during the California Gold Rush of 1849, then hit a new wave of popularity in the middle of the 20th century. Now the tang of sourdough is a favourite addition to many breads, from waffles to English muffins to rye bread, and the most popular, a dense sourdough French bread.
Making and maintaining your own sourdough starter is not difficult. A pot of starter takes at least a few days to ferment and develop a sour flavour before you add it to the first loaf, but after that, it can be used and replenished daily.

INGREDIENTS

250 ml (9 fl oz) low-fat milk, scalded
250 ml (9 fl oz) hot water
1 tbsp sugar
2¼ tsp active dry yeast
615 g (1 lb 6 oz) all-purpose flour or bread flour

METHOD

Mix the milk, water and sugar. When the temperature has cooled to between 40°C (105°F) and 46°C (115°F), add the yeast. Allow the yeast to develop a foamy head, a process that takes 5 to 10 minutes. Then add it to the flour and mix well.

Put the bowl in a warm place, between 27°C (80°F) and 39°F (100°F), like the back of the stove. Loosely cover the bowl so that air will still circulate and the starter will gather airborne yeasts. Within 24 hours, it should be bubbly and have the beginnings of a sour smell. Stir it once or twice a day. The starter may separate into a thick, curd-like mixture on the bottom and grey watery liquids on the top. That's normal, as long as it doesn't turn green or pink. (If it does, throw it out and start

again.) The mixture is ready to use when it develops a good sour smell, usually three to five days.

To bake sourdough bread, you need to prepare a sponge at least six hours in advance. Mix some starter with a portion of flour and liquid, as directed by the recipe. Replenish the starter with amounts of flour and water equal to the amount you removed. For instance, if the recipe calls for 125 ml (4 fl oz) of sourdough starter, replenish the starter with 125 ml (4 fl oz) water and 115 g (4 oz) flour. Both the sponge and the replenished starter should be put in a warm place, covered loosely and left to ferment at least 6 hours, until bubbly.

If you use the sourdough on an almost daily basis, you can leave the starter pot at the back of the stove, replenishing it after each use. It you are only an occasional baker, replenish it, let it sit out 6 to 24 hours, then put the starter in the refrigerator. The starter pot should be tightly covered when it is in the refrigerator. If you do not bake at least once a week, refresh the starter every week or two. Remove 250 ml (9 fl oz) of starter and discard the rest. Add 250 ml (9 fl oz) of water and 250 g (9 oz) of flour and return it to the refrigerator.

SOURDOUGH WALNUT RYE BREAD

This bread is good for meat or cheese sandwiches. Use walnut oil if you have it, otherwise substitute vegetable oil. Because the bread uses sourdough starter, the sponge should be made the night before baking.

450 g (1 lb) LOAF	INGREDIENTS	675 g (1½ lb) LOAF
125 ml (4 fl oz)	sourdough starter	185 ml (6½ fl oz)
100 ml (3½ fl oz)	water	175 ml (6 fl oz)
1 tbsp	walnut or vegetable oil	1½ tbsp
1 tbsp	sugar	1½ tbsp
1 tsp	salt	1½ tsp
2 tbsp	cornmeal	3 tbsp
250 g (9 oz)	rye flour	365 g (13 oz)
250 g (9 oz)	bread flour	365 g (13 oz)
2 tsp	yeast	1 tbsp
50 g (2 oz)	chopped walnuts	75 g (3 oz)

METHOD

To make sponge, combine sourdough starter, 60 ml (2 fl oz) of the water and 115 g (4 oz) of the rye flour. Stir well. Cover it loosely and set it in a warm place to ferment overnight.

Put the sponge and all remaining ingredients except walnuts in bread tin in order suggested by your bread machine instructions. Set for whole-wheat bread, medium crust. Press Start. Add walnuts after the first kneading or at the beeper.

SOURDOUGH RYE BREAD

This rye bread makes great sandwiches. It can be baked in the bread machine, but is also good baked in the oven.

450 g (1 lb) LOAF	INGREDIENTS	675 g (1½ lb) LOAF
60 ml (2 fl oz)	sourdough starter	90 ml (3 fl oz)
175 ml (6 fl oz)	water	250 ml (9 fl oz)
185 ml (6½ oz)	rye flour	270 g (10 oz)
2 tsp	caraway seeds	1 tbsp
1 tbsp	vegetable oil	1½ tsp
1 tbsp	sugar	1½ tbsp
1 tsp	salt	1½ tsp
400 g (15 oz)	bread flour	500 g (1 lb 2 oz)
2 tsp	yeast	1 tbsp

METHOD

The night before baking bread, make a sponge by combining the sourdough starter, 80 ml (3 fl oz) water (125 ml (4 fl oz), for larger loaf), rye flour and 1 tsp caraway seeds. Cover loosely and set in a warm place for at least 8 hours.

Put sponge and remaining ingredients in a bread tin in order suggested by your bread machine instructions. Set for whole-wheat bread, medium crust. Press Start.

To bake bread in a conventional oven, set the machine for the dough stage. Remove when dough is ready, punch down. Shape into a long, fat loaf or a round loaf. Place on a baking sheet slightly sprinkled with cornmeal. Cover loosely and put in a warm place to rise until doubled in volume, about 1 hour.

When bread has risen, make a wash of 1 lightly beaten egg and 1 tbsp water. Lightly brush the wash over the surface of the loaf, taking care not to deflate the dough. Bake bread in a preheated 180°C/350°F/Gas 4 oven until bread is crusty and makes a hollow sound when thumped on the top and bottom.

SOURDOUGH WHOLE-WHEAT BREAD

This is a dense and flavourful bread, but is not a high-riser.

450g (1lb) LOAF	INGREDIENTS	675g (1½ lb) LOAF
80 ml (3 fl oz)	sourdough starter	125 ml (4 fl oz)
80 ml (3 fl oz)	water	125 ml (4 fl oz)
40 g (1½ oz)	cracked wheat	60 g (2¼ oz)
2 tbsp	butter	3 tbsp
1 tbsp	honey	1½ tbsp
2 tbsp	dried milk	3 tbsp
1 tsp	salt	1½ tsp
250 g (9 oz)	bread flour	365 g (13 oz)
250 g (9 oz)	whole-wheat flour	365 g (13 oz)
1½ tsp	yeast	2¼ tsp

METHOD

The night before making bread, make the sponge by mixing sourdough starter, 115 g (4 oz) bread flour and about 2 tbsp water. Cover loosely and put in a warm place for at least 6 hours.

About 20 minutes before starting bread, put the cracked wheat in a small saucepan. Cover with water. Bring to a boil, then boil 6 minutes. Drain the wheat thoroughly, then let it cool at least 10 minutes.

Stir down the sponge and put it in the bread machine tin with the remainder of the water. Add cooled wheat and remaining ingredients in the order suggested by your bread machine instructions. Set for whole-wheat bread, medium crust. Press Start.

RIGHT Sourdough Whole-Wheat Bread

SOURDOUGH FRENCH BREAD

Sourdough bread can be both stubborn and temperamental, but it is also delicious. Unlike most of the other sourdough recipes in this book, the sourdough starter in this bread is a major ingredient, not just a small addition for extra flavour. The flavour will vary according to the type of sourdough starter you use and the airborne wild yeasts in your area. Because the sponge sits out for at least eight hours and absorbs moisture from the air, the amount of water you add may also vary.

450 g (1 lb) LOAF	INGREDIENTS	675 g (1½ lb) LOAF
175 ml (6 fl oz)	sourdough starter	250 ml (9 fl oz)
60 ml (2 fl oz)	water	90 ml (3 fl oz)
2 tsp	sugar	1 tbsp
1 tsp	salt	1½ tsp
415 g (15½ oz)	bread flour	575 g (1 lb 5 oz)
2 tsp	yeast	1 tbsp
1 tsp	cornstarch	1½ tsp
2 tbsp	water	3 tbsp

METHOD

The day before you bake the bread, make the sponge by mixing the starter, 165 g (6½ oz) flour and 2 tbsp water. Cover loosely and put in a warm place. Let sit at least 8 hours.

Put sponge, 2 tbsp water, sugar, salt, remaining flour and yeast in bread tin in order suggested by your bread machine instructions. Set for French or white bread, dough stage. Press Start.

When dough is ready, remove from bread machine and punch down. Shape the dough into one short, fat loaf, one round loaf, or one baguette for the smaller recipe, two baguettes for the large one. Place loaf on baking sheet that has been sprinkled with cornmeal. Use a sharp knife to cut several diagonal slashes in the top. Cover bread loosely and set it in a warm place to rise. This is a slow-rising bread which may take an hour or longer.

Preheat oven to 200°C/400°F/Gas 6. When bread has risen, dissolve cornstarch in 2 tbsp water and lightly brush it over the surface of the bread. For crustier bread, place a shallow pan of boiling water on the bottom shelf of the oven, or use a spray bottle to squirt water into the oven several times while baking. Bake 35 to 40 minutes, until crust is browned and bread makes hollow sound on top and bottom when rapped with knuckles.

COFFEE CAKES, SWEET BREADS AND DOUGHNUTS

CINNAMON STICKY BUNS

These sweet, sticky buns can be assembled in advance and refrigerated overnight. In the morning, they will have to finish their second rising before you bake them.

MAKES 15	INGREDIENTS	MAKES 22
	DOUGH	
125 ml (4 fl oz)	milk	210 ml (7 fl oz)
1	egg	1
3 tbsp	butter	4½ tbsp
40 g (1½ oz)	sugar	60 g (2¼ oz)
½ tsp	salt	¾ tsp
500 g (1 lb 2 oz)	bread flour	750 g (1 lb 11 oz)
2 tsp	yeast	1 tbsp
	FILLING	
50 g (2 oz)	brown sugar	85 g (3 oz)
1 tsp	cinnamon	1½ tsp
2 tbsp	very soft butter	3 tbsp
	SYRUP	
3 tbsp	butter	4½ tbsp
100 g (3½ oz)	brown sugar	165 g (6½ oz)
2 tbsp	water	3 tbsp
30	pecan halves	44

METHOD

Put dough ingredients in bread tin in order suggested by your bread machine instructions. Set for white or sweet bread, dough stage. Press Start.

Remove the dough from the bread machine and punch down. Let it rest for 5 minutes to make it easier to roll out. While dough is relaxing, mix brown sugar and cinnamon to make filling. For 450 g (1 lb) recipe, roll dough into a rectangle 18 cm (7 in) to 20 cm (8 in) wide and about 40.5 cm (16 in) long. For larger recipe, cut down in half and roll into two rectangles, each

18 cm (7 in) to 20 cm (8 in) wide and 28 cm (11 in) to 30 cm (12 in) long. Spread the soft butter over the surface of the dough. Thickly sprinkle brown sugar and cinnamon over the surface, spreading to edges. Roll dough into a long cylinder or cylinders. Slicing crosswise through the cylinder, cut into 15 pieces for the smaller recipe, 22 pieces for the larger.

The rolls can be baked together in baking tins or separately in muffin tins. The muffin tin rolls are neater and crusty on the outside. If you cook them in baking tins, they will be softer. A 20 × 20 cm (8 × 8 in) square baking pan is the perfect size for nine rolls; a 23 × 33 cm (9 × 13 in) tin should hold 15 rolls.

Make the syrup by combining butter, brown sugar and water in a small pan. Heat until butter is melted and sugar is dissolved. Stir well, then pour syrup into the bottoms of the baking tins or muffin tins. Place two pecan halves in the bottom of each muffin tin, or on the top of each roll if you are using baking tins. Place rolls in muffin tins, or turn them upside down (so pecans are on the bottom) in baking tins. Cover rolls loosely, set them in a warm place and let them rise until doubled, 45 minutes to 1 hour.

Bake rolls in a preheated 180°C/350°F/Gas 4 oven until they are nicely browned, 17 to 22 minutes in muffin tins, 20 to 25 minutes in baking tin. The rolls must be removed from the tins immediately, or the sugar syrup will harden. Keeping in mind that excess sugar syrup will run off, invert the tins or muffin tins over a large plate or baking sheet. Let them cool slightly, or the hot sugar will burn your mouth.

KUGELHOPF

This is an Austrian bread reputedly brought to France by Marie Antoinette. It is a sweet, fruit-studded batter bread and will not cook evenly in the bread machine, so must be baked in the oven. It is considered so special a bread that a fluted tube tin was created for it, but a bundt tin or angel food cake tin will do nicely.

450 g (1 lb) LOAF	INGREDIENTS	675 g (1½ lb) LOAF
2 + 1 yolk	eggs	4 eggs
45 ml (1½ fl oz)	milk	80 ml (3 fl oz)
75 g (3 oz)	butter	115 g (4 oz)
30 g (1½ oz)	sugar	50 g (2 oz)
½ tsp	vanilla	1 tsp
2 tsp	grated lemon peel	1 tbsp
½ tsp	salt	1 tsp
500 g (1 lb 2 oz)	bread flour	750 g (1 lb 11 oz)
2 tsp	yeast	1 tbsp
100 g (3½ oz)	raisins	165 g (6½ oz)
50 g (2 oz)	slivered almonds	100 g (3½ oz)
	confectioner's sugar	

METHOD

Put all ingredients except raisins, almonds and confectioner's sugar in bread tin in order suggested by your bread machine instructions. Set for white or sweet bread, dough stage. Press Start. Add raisins and almonds at the beeper or after the first kneading.

Remove the dough from the bread machine and punch down. Let it rest for 5 minutes. Butter a 1.5 l (54 fl oz) tube tin for the smaller loaf, a 2.25 l (81 fl oz) tube tin for the larger loaf. Put the dough in the tin and spread it around evenly. Cover loosely and put in a warm place to rise 45 minutes to 1 hour.

Bake kugelhopf in a preheated 180°C/350°F/Gas 4 oven until a skewer inserted in bread comes out clean, 35 to 40 minutes. Let cool 10 minutes, then invert on cooling rack. Dust with confectioner's sugar while kugelhopf is still warm.

ORANGE MONKEY BREAD

This sweet pull-apart bread is a favourite breakfast treat. Small balls of sweet, orange-flavoured dough are dipped in a melted butter seasoned with orange liqueur, dipped in cinnamon and sugar and layered in a baking tin. The bread is wonderful when warm, but still tastes good at room temperature. Time the making of the bread so it comes out of the oven 10 to 15 minutes before meal time.

450 g (1 lb) LOAF	INGREDIENTS	675 g (1½ lb) LOAF
175 ml (6 fl oz)	milk	250 ml (9 fl oz)
2 tbsp	butter	3 tbsp
2 tbsp	sugar	3 tbsp
½ tsp	salt	¾ tsp
2 tsp	grated orange peel	1 tbsp
500 g (1 lb 2 oz)	bread flour	750 g (1 lb 11 oz)
1½ tsp	yeast	2¼ tsp
3 tbsp	melted butter	4½ tbsp
2 tbsp	orange liqueur or orange juice	3 tbsp
200 g (7 oz)	sugar	345 g (12½ oz)
1 tsp	cinnamon	1½ tsp

METHOD

Put first seven ingredients in bread tin in order suggested by your bread machine instructions. Set for white or sweet bread, dough stage. Press Start.

Lightly butter baking dish. A few minutes before dough is ready, melt butter. Stir in orange juice or orange liqueur. In a separate bowl, mix the cinnamon and sugar. Put about half of the cinnamon and sugar in another bowl. Each time you dip a buttery ball into the sugar, it will drip a little of the butter into the sugar, and the sugar will become hard to work with. Then replenish it with some of the reserved cinnamon and sugar.

Remove the dough from the bread machine and punch down. Roll dough into a thick log and cut it into 20 to 24 pieces for the small loaf, 30 to 36 pieces for the large loaf. Roll pieces of dough into balls (they do not need to be perfectly round). Dip each ball in butter-orange mixture, then in cinnamon-sugar and layer in baking pan. Note: the pieces in the first layer should be close but not touching to give them room to rise. On each succeeding layer, place balls so they overlap empty spaces on the layer beneath. You can put the assembled bread in the refrigerator the night before, and it will rise a little overnight. Let the dough return to room temperature and finish rising, then bake. Monkey bread is traditionally baked in a tube tin, 25.5 cm (10 in) across for the larger loaf, a 18 cm (7 in) or 20 cm (8 in) tin for the smaller loaf. However, it looks impressive and tastes just as good when baked in round casserole dishes, about 2.5 cm (1 in) smaller in diameter than the tube tins.

Drizzle any remaining butter and cinnamon-sugar over the dough in the pan. Cover it loosely, and put it in a warm place to rise. When bread has doubled in volume, about 30 to 40 minutes, put it in preheated 180°C/350°F/Gas 4 oven. Bake until bread is lightly browned and a skewer inserted in the bread comes out clean, about 25 to 30 minutes. Invert bread on serving plate, being very careful of the hot syrup that has collected at the bottom of the tin. (Drain off excess syrup first, if desired, or let the syrup run onto the plate.) Remove baking tin, let it cool a little and serve.

CINNAMON RAISIN SWIRL BREAD

This is an easy breakfast bread that tastes like cinnamon rolls, although it is not as gooey. It is delicious warm, and doesn't need butter. The bread can be assembled the night before, then left to rise in the refrigerator overnight.

450 g (1 lb) LOAF	INGREDIENTS	675 g (1½ lb) LOAF
185 ml (6½ fl oz)	milk	270 ml (10 fl oz)
1 tbsp	butter	1½ tbsp
3 tbsp	sugar	4½ tbsp
1 tsp	salt	1½ tsp
500 g (1 lb 2 oz)	bread flour	750 g (1 lb 11 oz)
2 tsp	yeast	1 tbsp
40 g (1½ oz)	raisins	6 tbsp
1½ tbsp	very soft butter	2 tbsp
40 g (1½ oz)	brown sugar	6 tbsp
1 tsp	cinnamon	1½ tsp

METHOD

Put first six ingredients in bread tin in order suggested by your bread machine instructions. Set for white or sweet bread, dough stage. Press Start. Add the raisins after the first kneading or when the beep sounds to add fruit.

Remove butter from refrigerator to soften it. Mix brown sugar and cinnamon. Butter a 24 cm (9½ in) loaf tin (large enough for either recipe).

Remove dough from bread machine and punch down. Let it rest 5 minutes. Roll it out on a lightly floured surface to form a rectangle about 20 cm (8 in) wide and about 40 cm (16 in) long. Spread the butter then sprinkle the brown sugar mixture over the surface of the dough. Roll it into a fat, 20 cm (8 in) long cylinder. Tucking the edge under, put it in the loaf tin. Loosely cover and put in a warm place to rise for 1 hour.

Bake the loaf in a preheated 180°C/350°F/Gas 4 oven until top is golden and a skewer inserted in the bread comes out clean, 25 to 30 minutes. Remove the bread from the pan and put it on a wire rack. Let it cool at least 30 minutes so the hot sugar does not burn you.

BEIGNETS

These small, diamond-shaped doughnuts are a staple in New Orleans, where they are traditionally eaten warm with café au lait.

MAKES 4 DOZEN	INGREDIENTS	MAKES 6 DOZEN
175 ml (6 fl oz)	milk	270 ml (10 fl oz)
1	egg	1
½ tsp	vanilla	¼ tsp
2 tbsp	butter	3 tbsp
40 g (1½ oz)	sugar	60 g (2¼ oz)
½ tsp	salt	¼ tsp
¼ tsp	nutmeg	½ tsp
615 g (1 lb 6 oz)	bread flour	915 g (2 lb 2 oz)
1½ tsp	yeast	2¼ tsp

oil for frying

confectioner's sugar

METHOD

Put all ingredients except oil and confectioner's sugar in bread tin in order suggested by your bread machine instructions. Set for white bread, dough stage. Press Start.

When dough is ready, punch down. Let it rest about 5 minutes. Then, on a lightly floured surface, roll dough into a rectangle about 1 cm (½ in) thick. Working at a diagonal to the edge of the rectangle, cut dough into 4 cm (1½ in) strips. Then cut the strips into diamonds with a new series of cuts, almost but not quite perpendicular to the first. Place the diamonds on ungreased baking sheets. Cover loosely and put them in a warm place to rise for 45 minutes.

Pour oil at least 7.5 cm (3 in) deep into a deep frying pan, wok, or saucepan. Heat oil to 180°C (365°F). Watch the oil temperature carefully, as it can climb quickly. Slide a few beignets into the hot oil. Do not crowd them. They will bob back up to the surface. Cook until golden on the bottom, 2 to 3 minutes. Then turn and cook another 2 to 3 minutes on the other side. You may need to hold the beignets down with a large spoon or other cooking utensil to keep them from turning uncooked side up again.

When beignets are golden, remove them from the oil, letting them drain for a few moments over the oil. Then put them on several layers of paper towels. Sprinkle them with confectioner's sugar. Beignets should be served warm. You may put the cooked beignets in a warm oven while others are cooking. Make sure the oil temperature returns to 180°C (365°F) before you add the next batch of beignets.

CALAS

Calas are rice fritters made with a yeast dough and fried like small doughnuts. The grains of cooked rice disappear into the delicious puffs of fried dough.

MAKES 30	INGREDIENTS	MAKES 45
2	eggs	3
2 tsp	vanilla	1 tbsp
60 g (2¼ oz)	sugar	110 g (4 oz)
½ tsp	salt	¼ tsp
½ tsp	nutmeg	¼ tsp
½ tsp	grated lemon peel	¼ tsp
400 g (14 oz)	cooked, cooled rice	600 g (1 lb 6½ oz)
500 g (1 lb 2 oz)	bread flour	750 g (1 lb 11 oz)
1 tsp	yeast	1½ tsp
	oil for frying	
	confectioner's sugar	

METHOD

Put all ingredients except oil and confectioner's sugar in bread tin in order suggested by your bread machine instructions. Set for white bread, dough stage. Press Start.

When dough is ready, punch down. Let it rest about 5 minutes. Then cut off walnut-sized pieces and place them on a greased baking sheet. (Lightly flour your hands, if necessary, to work with the sticky batter.) Cover loosely and put them in a warm place to rise for 1 hour.

Pour oil at least 7.5 cm (3 in) deep into a deep frying pan, wok, or saucepan. Heat oil to 180°C (365°F). Watch the oil temperature carefully, as it can climb quickly. Slide a few rice balls into the hot oil. Do not crowd them. They will bob back up to the surface. Cook until golden on the bottom, about 2 minutes. Then turn and cook another 2 minutes on the other side.

When fritters are golden, remove them from the oil, letting them drain for a few moments over the oil. Then put them on several layers on paper towels. Sprinkle them with confectioner's sugar. Calas should be served warm. You may put the cooked calas in a warm oven while others are cooking. Make sure the oil temperature returns to 180°C (365°F) before you add the next batch of calas.

RAISED DOUGHNUTS

*Coated in sugar or drizzled with a sugar glaze, these doughnuts
are delicious.*

MAKES 8-10	INGREDIENTS	MAKES 12-15
125 ml (4 fl oz)	milk	200 ml (7 fl oz)
1	egg	1
2 tbsp	butter	3 tbsp
40 g (1½ oz)	sugar	60 g (2¼ oz)
½ tsp	salt	¼ tsp
500 g (1 lb 2 oz)	bread flour	750 g (1 lb 11 oz)
1½ tsp	yeast	2¼ tsp
	oil for frying	

CHOICE OF SUGAR COATINGS

confectioner's sugar
granulated cinnamon and sugar
sugar glaze (see below)

SUGAR GLAZE

165 g (6½ oz) confectioner's sugar
½ tsp vanilla
1 tbsp warm milk

METHOD

Put all ingredients except oil and sugar coating in bread tin in order suggested by your bread machine instructions. Set for white bread, dough stage. Press Start.

When dough is ready, punch down. Let it rest about 5 minutes. Then, on a lightly floured surface, roll dough into a rectangle about 4 mm (⅜ in) thick. Using a doughnut cutter or a 7.5 cm (3 in) biscuit cutter, cut out doughnuts. If you are not using a doughnut cutter, cut out a 1 cm (½ in) hole in the centre. Knead scraps together and let rest 5 minutes. Reroll the dough and cut out more doughnuts. Place the doughnuts on ungreased baking sheets. Cover loosely and put them in a warm place to rise 45 minutes to 1 hour, until doubled in bulk.

About 15 minutes before doughnuts finish rising, pour oil at least 7.5 cm (3 in) deep into a deep frying pan, wok, or saucepan. Heat oil to 185°C (365°F). Watch the oil temperature carefully, as it can climb quickly. Slide two or three doughnuts into the hot oil. Do not crowd them. Cook until golden on the bottom, 1½ to 2½ minutes. Then turn and cook the other side.

When doughnuts are golden, remove them from the oil, letting them drain for a few moments over the oil. Then put them on several layers of paper towels. Make sure the oil temperature returns to 185°C (365°F) before you add the next batch of doughnuts.

Put confectioner's sugar or a mixture of cinnamon and granulated sugar in a paper bag with two doughnuts. Shake until they are coated. Remove and repeat until all doughnuts are coated.

Alternatively, mix the ingredients for the sugar glaze together and drizzle it over the tops of the doughnuts.

KOLACHE

Kolaches are individual Czechoslovakian pastries with fruit or cheese fillings, often eaten at Easter or Christmas. Below are recipes for two fillings, or you can use your favourite recipe for other fruit, nut or poppyseed fillings. For special occasions, serve a variety of fillings.

MAKES 16	INGREDIENTS	MAKES 24
1	egg	1 + 1 yolk
125 ml (4 fl oz)	milk	185 ml (6½ fl oz)
50 g (2 oz)	butter	85 g (3 oz)
40 g (1½ oz)	sugar	60 g (2¼ oz)
½ tsp	salt	¾ tsp
500 g (1 lb 2 oz)	bread flour	750 g (1 lb 11 oz)
1½ tsp	yeast	2¼ tsp

confectioner's sugar

APRICOT FILLING
(Makes enough for 16 kolaches)

100 g (3½ oz) chopped dried apricots

50 g (2 oz) sugar

2 tbsp apricot brandy, orange liqueur or orange juice

CHEESE FILLING
(Makes enough for 24 kolaches)

75 g (3 oz) cream cheese, softened

130 g (4½ oz) ricotta cheese, watery liquids poured off

1 egg yolk

3 tbsp sugar

½ tsp fresh lemon juice

METHOD

Put all ingredients in bread tin in order suggested by your bread machine instructions. Set for white bread, dough stage. Press Start.

Lightly oil two baking sheets.

When dough is ready, remove from bread machine and punch down. Cut smaller recipe into 16 equal pieces, the larger recipe into 24 pieces. Roll each piece into a ball and flatten slightly. Place balls about 2.5 cm (1 in) apart in baking tin. Cover loosely and set in a warm place to rise until doubled, about 45 minutes.

Preheat oven to 190°C/375°F/Gas 5. Gently use one finger to make an indentation in the top of each kolache, taking care not to deflate the roll. Gently widen the hole with your finger. Put about 1 tbsp of filling (see below) in each kolache. Bake until kolaches are golden brown, 15 to 20 minutes. Sprinkle with confectioner's sugar while still warm.

APRICOT FILLING

Put apricots in a small saucepan. Cover with water. Bring to a boil, then reduce heat to very low. Simmer until water evaporates, watching closely and stirring frequently so apricots do not scorch. Just as last bit of water evaporates, add sugar and liqueur and heat just until sugar dissolves, about 1 minute. Let cool slightly, then purée in blender or food processor.

CHEESE FILLING

Beat all ingredients together until smooth.

SOPAIPILLAS

These Mexican treats are coated with sugar and served with honey.

MAKES 16	INGREDIENTS	MAKES 25
80 ml (3 fl oz)	water	125 ml (4 fl oz)
80 ml (3 fl oz)	milk	125 ml (4 fl oz)
1 tbsp	lard or solid shortening	1½ tbsp
1 tbsp	sugar	1½ tbsp
½ tsp	salt	¾ tsp
500 g (1 lb 2 oz)	bread flour	750 g (1 lb 11 oz)
1½ tsp	yeast	2¼ tsp
	oil for frying	
	confectioner's sugar	

METHOD

Put all ingredients except oil and confectioner's sugar in bread tin in order suggested by your machine's instructions. Set for white bread, dough stage. Press Start.

When dough is ready, punch down. Let it rest about 5 minutes. Then, on a lightly floured surface, roll dough into a rectangle about 4 mm (⅛ in) thick. Cut dough into 5 cm (2 in) squares. Place squares on ungreased baking sheets. Cover loosely and put in a warm place to rise while you heat the oil, about 15 minutes.

Pour oil at least 7.5 cm (3 in) deep into a deep frying pan, wok, or saucepan. Heat oil to 180°C (350°F). Watch the oil temperature carefully, as it can climb quickly. Slide a few sopaipillas into the hot oil. Do not crowd them. Cook until golden, turning once. Total cooking time is 1½ to 2 minutes.

Remove sopaipillas from the oil, letting them drain for a few moments. Then put them on several layers on paper towels. Sprinkle with confectioner's sugar, or put sugar and sopaipillas in a paper bag and shake. Make sure the oil temperature returns to 180°C (350°F) before you add the next batch.

PECAN CRESCENT ROLLS

With pecans, brown sugar and cinnamon, these sweet rolls are irresistible.

MAKES 16	INGREDIENTS	MAKES 24
1	egg	1
175 ml (6 fl oz)	milk	270 ml (10 fl oz)
50 g (2 oz)	butter	85 g (3 oz)
40 g (1½ oz)	sugar	60 g (2¼ oz)
½ tsp	salt	¾ tsp
615 g (1½ lb)	bread flour	915 g (2 lb 2 oz)
2 tsp	yeast	1 tbsp
FILLING		
2 tbsp	very soft butter	3 tbsp
50 g (2 oz)	brown sugar	85 g (3 oz)
1 tsp	cinnamon	1½ tsp
100 g (3½ oz)	finely chopped pecans	125 g (5 oz)

METHOD

Put all dough ingredients in bread tin in order suggested by your bread machine instructions. Set for white or sweet bread, dough stage. Press Start.

When dough is ready, remove it from the bread machine and punch it down. Cut the 450 g (1 lb) recipe in two equal parts, the larger recipe into three parts. Let the dough rest for 5 minutes. Oil two or three baking sheets.

On a lightly floured surface, roll out each section of dough into a circle, about 20 cm (8 in) in diameter. Spread surface with soft butter and sprinkle with mixed cinnamon and sugar, and pecans.

Cut each circle into eight wedges. Starting from the outside of the circle, loosely roll up each wedge toward the point. Stretch slightly and pull it into a curve. Set on the baking sheet with the point underneath.

Let the dough rise until doubled, about 1 hour. Bake in preheated oven 190°C/375°F/Gas 5, 12 to 15 minutes.

APPLE KUCHEN

Kuchen is an easy fruit-filled German coffee cake. This recipe is for an apple topping, but you can substitute soft fruits such as peaches or apricots and skip cooking the fruit before baking.

450 g (1 lb) LOAF	INGREDIENTS	675 g (1½ lb) LOAF
1	egg	1
125 ml (4 fl oz)	milk	200 ml (7 fl oz)
50 g (2 oz)	butter	85 g (3 oz)
40 g (1½ oz)	sugar	60 g (2¼ oz)
½ tsp	salt	¼ tsp
500 g (1 lb 2 oz)	bread flour	750 g (1 lb 11 oz)
1½ tsp	yeast	2¼ tsp
	TOPPING	
750 ml (27 fl oz)	peeled and sliced apples	1.1 l (40 fl oz)
1 tsp	fresh lemon juice	1 tsp
50 g (2 oz)	bread flour or all-purpose flour	85 g (3 oz)
50 g (2 oz)	sugar	75 g (3¼ oz)
1 tsp	cinnamon	1½ tsp
2 tbsp	butter, softened	3 tbsp

METHOD

Put all dough ingredients in bread tin. Set for white or sweet bread, dough stage. Press Start.

Make the fruit topping while bread machine is working. Pre-cook the apples slightly to soften them. Put them in a saucepan with the lemon juice and about 6 ml (2 fl oz) water. Bring water to a boil, then reduce heat and simmer apples, stirring frequently, until they are barely soft, 7 to 10 minutes. Add a little water if needed so apples don't scorch, but there should be as little liquid as possible in the pan when apples are done.

In the meantime, mix the flour, sugar and cinnamon. When apples are done, toss them with about 3 tbsp of the topping. Mix the softened butter with the rest of the topping. Set apples and topping aside until dough is ready.

Butter a 25.5 cm (10 in) round tin (I like to use a springform tin) or a 23 cm (9 in) square baking tin for the smaller recipe, two 20 cm (8 in) round tins for the larger one. When dough is ready, remove from tin and punch down. Let it rest 5 minutes. Roll dough out to fit baking tin or tins. Pat the dough into the bottom of the baking tin. Arrange apples on top of the dough. Sprinkle topping over apples. Cover kuchen and put it in a warm place to rise 15 to 20 minutes. Preheat oven to 180°C/350°F/Gas 4. (The short rising period will produce a denser, chewier dough. A longer rising period will produce a lighter, more bread-like dough.) Bake kuchen until edges of cake are golden brown, 30 to 35 minutes.

HOLIDAY BREADS

THREE KINGS BREAD

Three Kings Bread, or Rosca de los Reyes, is eaten in Mexico and Puerto Rico on Twelfth Night, January 6, the day the three kings brought Jesus gifts. A tiny ceramic doll, coin or lima bean may be hidden in the bread. The person who finds it throws a party on Candle Mass, February 2.

450 g (1 lb) LOAF	INGREDIENTS	675 g (1½ lb) LOAF
1	egg	1 + 1 yolk
125 ml (4 fl oz)	water	185 ml (6½ fl oz)
2 tbsp	powdered milk	3 tbsp
50 g (2 oz)	butter	85 g (3 oz)
3 tbsp	sugar	4½ tbsp
2 tsp	grated orange peel	1 tbsp
1 tsp	salt	1½ tsp
500 g (1 lb 2 oz)	bread flour	750 g (1 lb 11 oz)
2 tsp	yeast	1 tbsp
3 tbsp	chopped walnuts	4½ tbsp
2 tbsp	raisins	3 tbsp
3 tbsp	candied cherries	4½ tbsp

GLAZE

100 g (3½ oz) confectioner's sugar
1 tbsp milk or cream
¼ tsp vanilla

METHOD

Put all dough ingredients except fruit and nuts in bread tin in order suggested by your bread machine instructions. Set for white or sweet bread, dough stage. Press Start. Add fruit and nuts at beeper or after first kneading.

When dough is ready, remove from tin and punch down. Let it rest 5 minutes. Butter a 46 cm (18 in) baking sheet. Roll the bread into a rope, about 61 cm (24 in) for larger loaf. Bring ends of the rope together to form a ring, and place bread on baking sheet. Insert a ceramic doll, bean or foil-wrapped coin into the dough from the underside. Cover dough and put in a warm place to rise until doubled, 45 minutes to 1 hour.

Bake bread in preheated 200°C/400°F/Gas 6 oven until golden, about 25 minutes.

Make glaze by combining sugar, milk and vanilla. The glaze should be thin enough to drizzle it, but not runny. Adjust milk if necessary. When bread has cooled slightly but is still warm, drizzle the glaze over the ring.

Pan de Muertos (Bread of the Dead)

This sweet bread, flavoured with orange peel and anise seed and decorated with skull and crossbones, is traditionally eaten in Mexico on the Day of the Dead. This is a day of celebration in Mexico, when relatives honour the dead by visiting their graves and leaving flowers and food there. This bread is shaped and baked in a conventional oven. The dough will fit in either the 450 g (1 lb) or 675 g (1½ lb) bread machine.

INGREDIENTS

60 ml (2 fl oz) water	½ tsp anise seed
60 ml (2 fl oz) milk	750 g (1 lb 11 oz) bread flour
2 eggs	1 tbsp yeast
50 g (2 oz) butter	1 egg white
40 g (1½ oz) sugar	2 tbsp water
½ tsp salt	2 tsp sugar
1 tsp grated orange peel	¼ tsp cinnamon

METHOD

Put all but last four ingredients in bread tin in order suggested by your bread machine instructions. Set for white bread, dough stage. Press Start.

Grease a baking sheet. Make an egg wash by mixing the egg white and 2 tbsp water.

When dough is ready, remove it from the bread machine and punch down. Cut off about 50 g (2 oz) of dough. Shape the rest of the dough into a large, round loaf about 5 cm (2 in) high and place it on the baking sheet. Cut the small piece of dough into thirds. Roll two pieces between your palms to form skinny ropes. Flatten the ends a little so they look like bones. Dip them in the egg wash, then place them on top of the loaf in an X so they look like crossbones. Flatten the remaining piece of dough into a round, then pull it a little to elongate it so it looks like a skull. Dip it in the egg wash, then lightly press it onto the loaf, just above the crossbones. If desired, add tears or facial features.

Brush the loaf with egg wash. Cover the bread loosely. Set it in a warm place to rise until puffy, 30 to 45 minutes. Preheat oven to 190°C/375°F/Gas 5. Brush bread again with egg wash. Mix sugar and cinnamon and sprinkle over the bread. Bake until bread is browned and a little crusty, 30 to 35 minutes.

HOT CROSS BUNS

Hot Cross Buns, as an English tradition, are eaten on Good Friday. Without the cross, they make delicious breakfast rolls year-round.

450 g (1 lb) LOAF	INGREDIENTS	675 g (1½ lb) LOAF
1	egg	1 + 1 yolk
125 ml (4 fl oz)	milk	185 ml (6½ fl oz)
50 g (2 oz)	butter	75 g (3 oz)
40 g (1½ oz)	sugar	60 g (2¼ oz)
1 tsp	grated lemon peel	1½ tsp
½ tsp	cinnamon	¾ tsp
¼ tsp	nutmeg	½ tsp
⅛ tsp	ground cloves	¼ tsp
½ tsp	salt	¾ tsp
500 g (1 lb 2 oz)	bread flour	750 g (1 lb 11 oz)
2 tsp	yeast	1 tbsp
50 g (2 oz)	currants or raisins	85 g (3 oz)

GLAZE

100 g (3½ oz) confectioner's sugar
1 tbsp milk or cream
½ tsp lemon juice

METHOD

Put all ingredients except currants or raisins in bread tin in order suggested by your bread machine instructions. Set for white bread, dough stage. Press Start. Add the currants or raisins after the first kneading or when the machine signals it's time to add fruit.

Lightly oil a 23 cm (9 in) square tin or 25.5 cm (10 in) round tin for the smaller loaf, a 23 × 33 cm (9 × 13 in) tin or two 20 × 20 cm (8 × 8 in) square tins for the larger recipe.

When dough is ready, remove from bread machine and punch down. Cut smaller recipe into 12 to 16 equal pieces, the larger recipe into 18 to 24 pieces. Roll each piece into a ball. Place balls about 1 cm (½ in) apart in baking pan. Cover loosely and set in a warm place to rise until doubled, 45 minutes to 1 hour.

Preheat oven to 190°C/375°F/Gas 5. With a sharp knife or razor blade, cut a cross in the top of each roll. Bake 12 to 15 minutes, until a skewer inserted in roll comes out clean.

Make glaze, adding sugar or milk if needed to give it a consistency that will allow you to drizzle it over the rolls but is not runny. Let rolls cool slightly but not completely. Drizzle icing in a cross, following the cuts in the top of the bun.

PANETTONE

This is an Italian Christmas bread distinguished by its tall, domed shape.

450 g (1 lb) LOAF	INGREDIENTS	675 g (1½ lb) LOAF
60 ml (2 fl oz)	milk	6 tbsp
2	eggs	3
3 tbsp	butter	4½ tbsp
3 tbsp	sugar	4½ tbsp
½ tsp	salt	¾ tsp
1 tsp	grated lemon peel	1½ tsp
1 tsp	vanilla	1½ tsp
½ tsp	anise seed	¾ tsp
500 g (1 lb 2 oz)	bread flour	750 g (1 lb 11 oz)
2 tsp	yeast	1 tbsp
3 tbsp	pine nuts	4½ tbsp
2 tbsp	golden raisins	3 tbsp
40 g (1½ oz)	chopped candied fruit	60 g (2¼ oz)
1 tbsp	flour	1 tbsp

METHOD

Put all ingredients except pine nuts, raisins, fruit and the last tablespoon of flour in bread tin in order suggested by your bread machine instructions. Set for white bread, dough stage. Press Start.

The high sugar content interferes with the rising action of the yeast, so it is kneaded after the first rising. Remove the dough and punch down. Toss candied fruit with 1 tbsp flour, then gently knead the fruit, raisins and pine nuts into the dough. Put the dough in a buttered tin and turn to grease sides. Panettone is traditionally baked in a tall, cylindrical tin. Use a 450 g (1 lb) coffee tin or a 1.25 l (45 fl oz) soufflé dish for the smaller loaf and a slightly oversized loaf tin or a 2 l (72 fl oz) round casserole dish for the larger one. Set it in a warm place, cover loosely, and let rise until doubled in volume.

Bake in preheated 180°C/350°F/Gas 4 oven until golden and skewer inserted comes out clean, 30 minutes.

LEFT Panettone

CHALLAH

Challah is an egg bread that is oven-baked for the Jewish sabbath. It is usually a straight, plaited loaf, but sometimes the plait is coiled like a snail. At Rosh Hashanah, it may be formed in a circle, symbolizing a prayer rising heavenward.

450 g (1 lb) LOAF	INGREDIENTS	675 g (1½ lb) LOAF
2	eggs	3
60 ml (2 fl oz)	water	90 ml (3 fl oz)
1 tbsp	butter	1½ tbsp
2 tbsp	sugar	3 tbsp
1 tsp	salt	1½ tsp
500 g (1 lb 2 oz)	bread flour	750 g (1 lb 11 oz)
2 tsp	yeast	1 tbsp

GLAZE

1 egg yolk
1 tsp water
1–2 tsp poppy seeds

METHOD

Put ingredients in bread tin in order suggested by your bread machine instructions. Set for white bread, dough stage. Press Start.

When dough is ready, remove and punch down. Cut dough into three equal parts. Roll each piece into a rope about 30 cm (12 in) long for the small loaf, 40.5 cm (16 in) to 46 cm (18 in) for the large loaf. Plait the three ropes together. Pinch the ends together and turn them under. Cover the loaf and set it in a warm place to rise until doubled in volume, 45 minutes to 1 hour.

Preheat the oven to 180°C/350°F/Gas 4. Make glaze by beating egg yolk and water with fork. Brush lightly over loaf. Sprinkle top with poppy seeds.

Bake until top is nicely browned, 30 to 35 minutes.

VANOCKA
(CZECHOSLOVAKIAN CHRISTMAS BREAD)

This is a plaited loaf, seasoned with ginger and nutmeg and full of fruit and nuts. It takes some work to knead in the fruit and to make the elegant plaits. The loaf is baked in the oven. This recipe will fit both the 450 g (1 lb) and 657 g (1½ lb) tins.

INGREDIENTS

175 ml (6 fl oz) milk	1 tbsp yeast
1 egg	40 g (1½ oz) slivered
50 g (2 oz) butter	blanched almonds
50 g (2 oz) sugar	50 g (2 oz) golden raisins
1 tsp salt	1 tbsp candied orange peel
¼ tsp ground ginger	1 egg yolk beaten with 1 tbsp
¼ tsp ground nutmeg	water
1 tsp grated lemon peel	2 tbsp sliced almonds
750 g (1 lb 11 oz) bread flour	confectioner's sugar

METHOD

Put milk, egg, butter, sugar, salt, spices, lemon peel, flour and yeast in bread tin in order suggested by your bread machine instructions. Set for white or sweet bread, dough stage. Press Start. You may add the almonds when the machine signals time to add fruit, but don't add the raisins and candied orange peel because the additional sugar in an already sweet bread could interfere with the yeast's rising action.

Oil a baking sheet at least 36.5 cm (14 in) long. When the dough is ready, remove and punch down. Knead in the fruit and nuts. Cut the dough into four equal parts. Take three and roll each to form a rope about 46 cm (18 in) long. Plait the ropes, pinch ends together, and place on the baking sheet.

Cut the remaining piece into four equal parts. Again, take three and roll each between your hands to form a thin rope about 46 cm (18 in) long. Plait the ropes and centre the plait on top of the fat plait. Run wetted fingers along the underside of the thin plait, then lightly press it onto the fat plait. Pinch the ends together and press them under the ends of the fat plait.

Cut the remaining piece into two equal parts. Roll each into a skinny rope about 40.5 cm (16 in) long. Twist the two ropes together. Centre the twist on the thin braid. Wet your fingers and run them lightly on the underside of the twist, then lightly press onto the thin plait. Pinch the ends together and turn them under. Use four or five toothpicks to skewer the plaits in place. Otherwise, the top plaits may slip off as the dough rises. Cover bread loosely, put in a warm place and let rise until dough has almost doubled, about an hour.

Preheat the oven to 190°C/375°F/Gas 5. Lightly brush with the egg wash, then sprinkle the sliced almonds over the top and press a few into the sides. Bake until brown and a skewer inserted in a thick part comes out clean. Sprinkle with confectioner's sugar while warm.

MORAVIAN SUGAR BREAD

Moravian Sugar Bread is a coffee cake that originated in Germany and was brought to the United States by Moravians who settled in North Carolina.

450 g (1 lb) LOAF	INGREDIENTS	675 g (1½ lb) LOAF
5 tbsp	milk	125 ml (4 fl oz)
1	egg	1 + 1 yolk
75 g (3 oz)	mashed potatoes	115 g (4 oz)
3 tbsp	butter	4½ tbsp
40 g (1½ oz)	sugar	60 g (2¼ oz)
½ tsp	salt	¾ tsp
500 g (1 lb 2 oz)	bread flour	750 g (1 lb 11 oz)
1½ tsp	yeast	2¼ tsp
	TOPPINGS	
50 g (2 oz)	brown sugar	85 g (3 oz)
½ tsp	cinnamon	¾ tsp
¼ tsp	nutmeg	¼ tsp
3 tbsp	butter	4½ tbsp

METHOD

Put dough ingredients in bread tin in order suggested by your bread machine instructions. Use a 24 cm (9 in) loaf tin for the smaller loaf and a 23 × 23 cm (9 × 9 in) square baking tin for the larger one. Set for white or sweet bread, dough stage. Press Start.

When dough is ready, remove from bread machine and punch down. Put dough in a greased baking tin and turn so all sides of dough are greased. The mashed potatoes should be plain, with no butter, milk or seasonings. Cover, put in a warm place and let rise until doubled in bulk. Preheat oven to 190°C/375°F/Gas 5.

Make topping by combining all ingredients in a small saucepan. Heat, stirring often, until butter is melted and sugar is dissolved. With your fingertips, gently make shallow indentations all over the top of the dough. Spread topping across top of bread. Bake 30 minutes.

SWEDISH CHRISTMAS BREAD

This is a dark, dense rye bread made with stout or ale, flavoured with orange peel and molasses, and studded with bits of candied orange peel. It is best eaten simply with butter.

450 g (1 lb) LOAF	INGREDIENTS	675 g (1½ lb) LOAF
185 ml (6½ fl oz)	dark stout or ale	270 ml (10 fl oz)
1 tbsp	vegetable oil	1½ tbsp
3 tbsp	molasses	4½ tbsp
½ tsp	salt	¾ tsp
165 g (6½ oz)	bread flour	270 g (9 oz)
365 g (13 oz)	rye flour	550 g (1 lb 4 oz)
1 tbsp	grated orange peel	1½ tbsp
2 tsp	yeast	1 tbsp
2 tbsp	candied orange peel	3 tbsp

METHOD

Put all ingredients except candied orange peel in bread tin in order suggested by your bread machine instructions. Set for whole-wheat bread, medium crust. Add candied orange peel after first kneading or when beeper indicates time to add fruit.

GREEK NEW YEAR'S BREAD

This bread, slightly sweet and flavoured with orange, is traditionally eaten on New Year's Eve. The baker hides a coin in the bread, and the person who finds it will have good luck in the new year, according to Greek tradition.

450 g (1 lb) LOAF	INGREDIENTS	675 g (1½ lb) LOAF
1	egg	2 + 1 yolk
80 ml (3 fl oz)	milk	125 ml (4 fl oz)
50 g (2 oz)	butter	85 g (3 oz)
40 g (1½ oz)	sugar	60 g (2¼ oz)
2 tsp	grated lemon peel	1 tbsp
2 tsp	grated orange peel	1 tbsp
½ tsp	salt	¼ tsp
500 g (1 lb 2 oz)	bread flour	750 g (1 lb 11 oz)
2 tsp	yeast	1 tbsp

GLAZE

1 egg white beaten with 2 tsp water
2–3 tbsp pine nuts
(you may substitute slivered almonds)
1–2 tbsp sugar

METHOD

Put all dough ingredients in bread machine tin. Set for white or sweet bread, dough stage. Press Start.

When dough is ready, remove from tin and punch down. Let it rest 5 minutes. Butter a baking sheet. Roll the bread into a rope, about 84 cm (30 in) for smaller loaf, about 109 cm (40 in) for larger loaf. Coil the rope into a circle on the buttered baking sheet. Insert a foil-wrapped coin into the dough from the underside, where it cannot be seen. Cover dough and put in a warm place to rise until doubled, 45 minutes to 1 hour.

Brush dough with egg-water wash. Stick pine nuts in the folds of the dough, following the circular pattern. Sprinkle with sugar.

Bake bread in preheated 190°C/375°F/Gas 5 oven until golden, about 30 minutes.

INDEX